MUGGLENET.COM's
HARRY POTTER SHOULD HAVE DIED

MUGGLENET.COM's

HARRY POTTER SHOULD HAVE DIED

CONTROVERSIAL VIEWS FROM THE #1 FAN SITE

EMERSON SPARTZ
BEN SCHOEN
WITH JEANNE KIMSEY

Ulysses Press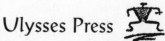

Published in the United States by
Ulysses Press
P.O. Box 3440
Berkeley, CA 94703
www.ulyssespress.com

ISBN: 978-1-56975-711-6
Library of Congress Control Number 2009902108

Contributing Writer: Jeanne Kimsey
Acquisitions Editor: Nick Denton-Brown
Managing Editor: Claire Chun
Copyeditors: Jennifer Privateer, Elyce Petker
Editorial Associates: Lauren Harrison, Rupa Ved
Production: Abigail Reser
Front cover design: Dylan Spartz

Printed in Canada by Webcom

8 10 9 8 7 6 5 4 3 2 1

Distributed by Publishers Group West

Table of Contents

Introduction

Harry Potter is *far* from being over. The final installment in the seven-part series may have been released two years ago, but fans are still waging fierce wars on the Internet and in coffee shops, picking sides on the many controversial issues left unresolved.

In the pages that follow, we investigate matters such as "Was Snape really a hero?" or "Should Voldemort be pitied or loathed?" and argue both sides. Then we tell you what we really think with a decisive verdict at the end of each debate.

We have a reputation for being very opinionated. In 2005, one of the authors (Emerson Spartz) nearly incited a rebellion in the fandom. He declared that fans who, after reading Book Five, *still* thought Hermione was going to be Harry's girlfriend were completely delusional. He was right, but his inbox filled up with death threats. To nobody's surprise, he thought they were hilarious, and he used them to create the infamous MuggleNet.com Wall of Shame.

So, if you have both a pulse and a passing knowledge of the Harry Potter books, we'll be very disappointed if, upon reading some of our verdicts, you're not inspired to challenge us to a duel or something.

We also have a unique perspective on these debates. Our website—the "Mighty MuggleNet" (as J.K.R. herself calls it)—is the most popular Harry Potter site in the world, receiving over 15 million hits per month. Emerson founded MuggleNet in 1999 when he was twelve years old, and Ben Schoen joined the team a few years later. Ben helps run the site and is a host on MuggleNet's popular podcast, MuggleSpace, which at one point had the distinction of being the #1 podcast on iTunes. MuggleNet contains hundreds of pages of information, discussions, movie clips, news articles, and more—anything you can possibly imagine that has to do with Harry Potter. The site is maintained by a volunteer staff of 120 passionate and dedicated Potter fans of all ages and nationalities. We've been huge fans since the beginning.

Combined, we've spent thousands of hours dissecting and investigating the Harry Potter novels.

It's a ton of work, but we love what we do. And there are *awesome* perks: We get to organize events that draw tens of thousands of fans, set up interviews and live chats with movie stars, cover and attend glitzy, star-studded movie premieres, and make sponsored visits to the movie sets! Fact: We are the *luckiest* fans in the entire world.

In 2007, we published our first book, *MuggleNet.com's What Will Happen in Harry Potter 7: Who Lives, Who Dies, and How the Series Finally Ends* (Ulysses Press). The book was a smashing success—it quickly became a *New York Times* bestseller and spent six months on the list. In the book, we made the following controversial (but correct) predictions:

Harry is a Horcrux.

Snape is working for Dumbledore.

Harry will live.

R.A.B. is Regulus Black.

Snape loved Lily.

The first prediction—we believed Harry was the seventh Horcrux—was very unpopular in the fan community. On our book tour, we spent most of our time at each bookstore facing a firing squad of fans challenging our theory, some even insulting our intelligence. But we stuck to our guns—the facts were on our side—and were eventually proven to be correct. So you can see how we are the kind of fans who would choose a title like *Harry Potter Should Have Died*. (For the record, this is Ben's contention—not Emerson's.)

Before each Harry Potter novel was released, fans argued passionately about what was going to happen. Now that the last book in the series has been released, fans are arguing passionately about what really happened, what should have happened, and what lessons can be learned. Far from being over, the Harry Potter legacy is still steaming ahead. It's impossible to ignore the issues that have kept the fandom going for more than a decade. This book tries to resolve these disputes.

We hope you enjoy our work, and we look forward to receiving your feedback on our website.

Abbreviations Used in Book

SS	*Harry Potter and the Sorcerer's Stone*
CoS	*Harry Potter and the Chamber of Secrets*
PoA	*Harry Potter and the Prisoner of Azkaban*
GoF	*Harry Potter and the Goblet of Fire*
OotP	*Harry Potter and the Order of the Phoenix*
HBP	*Harry Potter and the Half-Blood Prince*
DH	*Harry Potter and the Deathly Hallows*
FB	Fantastic Beasts and Where to Find Them
QA	Quidditch Through the Ages
BtB	Beedle the Bard
WB	Warner Brothers Studio
Marauders	James Potter, Sirius Black, Remus Lupin, and Peter Pettigrew
The Trio	Harry, Hermione, and Ron
J.K.R.	J. K. Rowling
JKR-AOL	AOL Chat. October 19, 2000.
JKR-BBC	BBC "Harry Potter and Me Christmas Special." December 28, 2001.
JKR-BC	Bloomsbury Chat. July 30, 2007.
JKR-BNY	Barnes and Noble Yahooligans Chat. October 20, 2000.
JKR-CH	Carnegie Hall interview. October 20, 2007.
JKR-CL	Connection with Christopher Lydon interview. October 12, 1999.
JKR-MN	MuggleNet interview. July 16, 2005.
JKR-MTV	MTV interview with Adler Shawn. October 15, 2007.
JKR-MTVC	MTV interview on Christian Imagery with Adler Shawn. October 17, 2007.
JKR-OS	J. K. Rowling's official website
JKR-PC1	Leaky Cauldron. "Pottercast 130: The One With Rowling." December 18, 2007.
JKR-PC2	Leaky Cauldron. "Pottercast 131: Rowling Along." December 24, 2007.
JKR-RCM	Radio City Music Hall Reading Second Night. August 2, 2006.
JKR-RN	Red Nose Day Chat. March 12, 2001.
JKR-TD	*Today Show* interview. July 26, 2007.
JKR-TD2	*Today Show* interview. July 29, 2007.
JKR-TD3	*Today Show* interview. July 30, 2007.
JKR-BDC	World Book Day Chat. March 4, 2004.
JKR-RI	Razia Iqbal interview. BBC News, November 1, 2007.

Should J.K. Rowling have kept Dumbledore's sexual orientation private?

No!

The controversy about Dumbledore's orientation all started in October 2007 at Carnegie Hall, when J.K.R. was asked if Albus Dumbledore had ever had true love with anyone in his long life. The author replied without hesitation that he was gay:

> I always thought of Dumbledore as gay [ovation from crowd]. ... Dumbledore fell in love with Grindelwald, and that added to his horror when Grindelwald showed himself to be what he was. To an extent, do we say it excused Dumbledore a little more because falling in love can blind us to an extent? But, he met someone as brilliant as he was, and rather like Bellatrix, he was very drawn to this brilliant person, and horribly, terribly let down by him. Yeah, that's how I always saw Dumbledore. In fact, recently I was in a script read through for the sixth film, and they had Dumbledore saying a line to Harry early in the script, saying I knew a girl once, whose hair... [laughter]. I had to write a little note in the margin and slide it along to the scriptwriter, 'Dumbledore's gay!' [laughter]. If I'd known it would make you so happy, I would have announced it years ago! [JKR-CH]

Although the crowd at Carnegie Hall cheered the news, the international press reacted like a bunch of Rita Skeeters (the tabloid journalist who penned a tell-all book about Dumbledore in DH), writing that his relationship with young Harry Potter was somehow immoral. Talking heads on TV wondered if the kindly old wizard was suddenly too shocking and controversial to be included in a book for children. Readers on fan forums and blogs moaned that the author had ruined their personal perception of Dumbledore because they had never thought of him as gay while reading the books.

But get over it—Jo is a strong, proud woman, and kudos to her for being honest! She created Professor Dumbledore, and he is a fabulous character who always stands up for the truth. And in this case, the fact is that Dumbledore never falls in love with a woman, he falls in love with a man. For J.K.R. to dance around that would have been dishonest and cowardly, and it would have sent the message that she was ashamed of the one gay character she created. And it doesn't change anything in the story one bit—Dumbledore can be gay and still be a wise and ethical advisor for Harry. He can be gay and still be a Gryffindor. In an interview with the BBC a few days after outing Dumbledore, J.K.R. said rather scornfully: "... do I think a gay person can be a moral compass? I think it's ludicrous that we're asking that in the 21st century." [JKR-RI] Exactly. People need to come into the 21st century and stop being so prudish.

Even though the religious right started jumping up and down raving about this issue as if Dumbledore were suddenly a monster, J.K.R. didn't bring up Dumbledore's orientation just to shock people or because sex is so important to the story. Obviously, it isn't since Dumbledore is over one hundred years old and as celibate as any priest. But the author had to explain why someone as intelligent as Dumbledore could have had a fatal attraction to a man like Grindelwald, who held racist beliefs and thought Muggles should be dominated by wizards. It was a youthful infatuation—one that was over with very quickly—but it's important to understand that Dumbledore's mistake was not in allowing himself a gay romance, but in trusting the wrong person. J.K.R.'s point is that love is blind. That is a lesson for people of every persuasion; it just so happens that in this case the relationship is gay.

Looking back, it's great to know that there was a major character in the books who had his own private struggles because his orientation was different. Now we know that a gay wizard can be a successful headmaster of Hogwarts, someone who never backs down from a fight, and who maintains his sense of humor and regal dignity no matter what. The Harry Potter books are sometimes dismissed as stereotypical for their emphasis on traditional marriage and family life, but Dumbledore had an alternate lifestyle all along. We should applaud J.K.R. for being bold and giving kids a role model—to make the smartest, most powerful wizard in the world gay sends a strong message and advances tolerance and equality. It also shows that discrimination isn't just between pureblood wizards and half-blood wizards. Bigotry exists in many forms.

Yes!

It would have been better if J.K.R. had never blurted out her view of Dumbledore's sexuality. Fans who never saw Dumbledore as a gay man were left feeling uneasy about having missed something, as if they had failed a test of political correctness set up by the author. J.K.R. may have thought of Dumbledore as gay all along, but she never bothered to ask her fans what they believed. Most people had honestly never given it much thought. After J.K.R. made her statement, the outrage didn't just come from homophobes or religious fanatics, but from parents who were taken aback that a children's author would bring up a controversial adult topic (which was rather understated in DH) and force it into the public light with all the media watching. Not everyone was thrilled to discuss the implications of a gay Dumbledore with underage children. Why didn't she just answer that Dumbledore had been in love once or twice and let people figure it out for themselves depending on their maturity level? Instead, J.K.R. went overboard and gave out too much information, just as she has repeatedly done about many other characters since DH came out. The truth is that Dumbledore's sexual preference is *not* that obvious in the books, and it is nearly irrelevant to the plot because friendship could have explained all his actions.

The author shouldn't be surprised that some fans never saw Dumbledore as gay since she gave us the information through a very unreliable narrator—Rita Skeeter. No one could miss the gay innuendos in her book about Dumbledore, but why should readers believe anything Rita writes? In GoF, Rita wrote insulting smears about Hagrid being a half-giant, and she completely invented a torrid love triangle between Harry, Hermione, and Viktor Krum. None of it was true! We know that one time she wrote a true story about Harry in OotP under threat of blackmail, but the rest of the time Rita was just a muckraker working for money. So most readers took what she wrote about Dumbledore and Grindelwald with a grain of salt, especially when she implied something unclean in the relationship between Dumbledore and Harry. We knew that part wasn't true, so why would we have believed any of it?

Gay readers themselves might have thanked J.K.R. more if she had introduced a gay character on the brighter side of one hundred years old who wasn't celibate and eccentric. In fact, many readers, gay and straight, saw more potential in the dashing Sirius Black since his main relationships in life were all with men, and he never married or had time for a girlfriend. In OotP, he is shown as a teenager ignoring a girl who is clearly interested in him. J.K.R. tried to put the rumor to rest in DH by letting Harry see pictures of Muggle girls in bathing suits on Sirius's bedroom wall at Grimmauld Place, but clever readers had a plausible answer for that: Sirius put those there to shock his pureblood mother, but he was also trying to fool his family into believing he was straight. Fan fiction writers have also insisted for years that Remus Lupin was gay, but the author married him off to femme fatale Nymphadora Tonks in DH. Yet that didn't stop the speculation because, after all, Lupin tried his best to abandon his wife and child, and he seemed sorry he ever got married to a woman at all. J.K.R. has always been aware that fans will ignore her views on a character's orientation and relationships, no matter what she says. If she chose not to resolve questions of sexual orientation in the books, then it would be better if she kept her views to herself and let the fans make up their own minds.

In discussing whether Dumbledore's sexuality is even relevant to the books, J.K.R. spoke to Leaky Cauldron's Pottercast about her perception of the relationship between Gellert Grindelwald and Dumbledore:

> How relevant is that to the books? Well, it's only relevant if
> you considered that his feelings for Grindelwald, as revealed in
> the 7th book, were an infatuation rather than a straightforward
> friendship. That's how I think—in fact, I know that some, perhaps
> sensitive, adult readers had already seen that. I don't think that
> came as a big surprise to some adult readers. I think a child would
> see a friendship, and a very devoted friendship. . . Dumbledore,
> who was the great defender of love, and who sincerely believed
> that love was the greatest, most powerful, force in the universe,
> was himself made a fool of by love. That to me was the interest-
> ing point. That in his youth, he was—he became infatuated with
> a man who was almost his dark twin. He was as brilliant, he was
> morally bankrupt, and Dumbledore lost his moral compass.

There's a lot in that statement to agitate readers. J.K.R. implies that people who didn't see Dumbledore as gay were insensitive or were too naïve to see it. And it's not exactly a message of tolerance that when Dumbledore allowed himself to love a male friend, he realized he was being a fool. Most of the time in the Harry Potter books, young love is the best of all possible emotions, and nearly every character meets a soul mate for life at an early age. Since Dumbledore is the only gay character, it's just totally negative that his soul mate turned into his dark evil twin. It was so devastating to Dumbledore that he basically never got over it, and he lived his life as an old, celibate, stereotypical British headmaster–type because of it. That is not a message of hope for the gay community, or for anyone.

J.K.R. compares Dumbledore with Bellatrix Lestrange, the obsessed Death Eater who is completely bewitched by Lord Voldemort. That's a really harsh comparison. Most readers think of Dumbledore as a leader instead of a follower, and it's obvious in the book that he broke away from Grindelwald after a very short time—about as long as Harry dated Cho Chang in OotP.

The story of Grindelwald and Dumbledore was about a friendship gone bad, and J.K.R. was wrong to insist that sexual attraction was the key. It's not a failure on the part of the readers if they didn't automatically assume that Dumbledore was gay.

Verdict

J. K. Rowling is a bold progressive who wanted the world to know that she wrote the character of Albus Dumbledore as a gay man. But opinions differ about the wisdom of outing an elderly character whose sexuality doesn't really matter much to the plot. Did Jo miss a big opportunity to write more openly about Dumbledore and Grindelwald without the smokescreen of Rita Skeeter's harsh prejudices? Or did J.K.R.'s statements leave a lasting legacy of tolerance that her gay readership will applaud for years to come? The verdict is: Absolutely—yes—it is important to the story, and J.K.R. was courageous for revealing the sexual orientation of this incredibly inspirational character.

Does Harry Potter die in Deathly Hallows?

No

Harry never truly dies in DH, although he comes close. The *Avada Kedavra* spell thrown by Voldemort can't kill Harry because Voldemort shares some of Harry's blood, which is protected by the unselfish death of Harry's mother, Lily. Voldemort takes the blood forcibly from Harry and uses it for his own return in GoF, which ironically means that he can no longer kill Harry, and therefore Harry never dies in the forest. The only part of him that dies and disappears is the Horcrux from the scar on his forehead. J.K. Rowling admits as much on her official site:

> Q: What exactly was the mutilated baby-like creature Harry saw at King's Cross in chapter 35 of "Hallows"?
>
> A: I've been asked this a LOT. It is the last piece of soul Voldemort possesses. When Voldemort attacks Harry, they both fall temporarily unconscious, and both their souls—Harry's undamaged and healthy, Voldemort's stunted and maimed—appear in the limbo where Harry meets Dumbledore.

Harry has already figured out nearly everything he and Dumbledore talk about, and he doesn't have to be in the afterlife to imagine he is seeing the train station and the deformed baby-crux that represents Voldemort. The horrible baby under the train bench is probably just a memory of the deformed cauldron baby from GoF, when Peter brings Voldemort back to his human form. Since Harry regains consciousness so quickly in the forest and his body is never under any sort of stress, there's no reason to think that Harry is ever completely dead.

Yes

If people die when their souls leave their body, then Harry is definitely dead. The trip to "King's Cross" seems like a dream, but throughout the books there is the message that souls are real and can move from place to place, even if a body is destroyed, which is how Voldemort survived so long after Harry vanquished him the first time. That's also the explanation for ghosts that choose to stay in the world and the spirits from the afterlife who must be summoned to return with the Resurrection Stone in DH. The *Avada Kedavra* is a powerful spell that cannot be blocked, and Harry doesn't even try to block it because he wants to protect his friends as his mother protected him with an unselfish sacrifice. So the result is that both his own soul and the piece of Voldemort's Horcrux that was lodged in his head are transported to another plane of existence for a few moments. Harry can see both himself and the crying baby, which is Voldemort's maimed and incomplete soul. It is the classic out-of-body experience when Harry enters a heavenly purgatory where he speaks to a wise mentor—in this case, Dumbledore. Since we know that Dumbledore's body was buried in the grave at Hogwarts, then what Harry sees has to be Dumbledore's soul made whole again. They are not on earth anymore, but Harry can touch Dumbledore's arm and it is real. Since Harry isn't very religious, there is no reason to think his subconscious mind would invent a heaven where souls are made. Why would his imagination conjure up the idea that in heaven he can see without his glasses, i.e., is made whole again? Harry would not have that belief in his subconscious, therefore, it must be actually happening to him and not part of a dream. Another clue that shows that Harry really dies is that Dumbledore gives him information that he never talks about during his life, such as his feelings for Gellert Grindelwald and the remorse he feels over the death of his sister Ariana. It is all very secret and personal, and Harry could never have guessed those details on his own. In the end, Harry is given a choice of whether to return to his body or move on, presumably to eternal life. He only wakes up when his soul chooses to go back into his body, and he is resurrected from the dead.

Verdict

Did Harry truly depart this world and pass on in DH, or was it all in his head? What seemed like just a dream could also be explained as Harry's soul leaving the body and going to heaven. But Harry was anchored to the earth by the very blood in Voldemort's veins, and the Avada Kedavra *spell merely killed the Horcrux in Harry's forehead. While it's a thin line between life and death, in this case the verdict is: No, Harry did not die in DH.*

Are the Slytherins too demonized?

No!

No way. The Slytherins are not demonized at all. It's just that Harry sees the world in black and white, and he has to grow up to see the shades of gray. Most of the Slytherins keep their best side hidden, and you have to look at what they do and not what they say. Whoever thought we'd be sympathetic to Severus Snape or Narcissa Malfoy? They turned out to be better people than we thought, which proves that Slytherins are just as human as the other characters and not the devils we thought we should fear.

Snape is the epitome of a Slytherin—dark, sarcastic, and cruel at times. Yet in the "Prince's Tale" told in DH, we learn that he started out in life just as innocently as Harry. He becomes a Death Eater, of course, but then he changes out of love for Lily Potter. Harry doesn't know that for most of the series, so he demonizes Snape and even wants to kill him. Yet once Harry finds out the truth, he forgives Snape, and that's the most important thing—even a Slytherin can be redeemed. Snape is the opposite of Peter Pettigrew, the Gryffindor who turns to the Dark Side, so we get a balanced view that none of the houses are all good or all bad.

Regulus Black, another Slytherin, is not demonic. He has a resemblance to his brother, Sirius, and that makes him an attractive character. He has Slytherin pride, but he also cares about Kreacher as much as Harry loves Dobby, and that gives him the guts to stand up to Voldemort in DH. That's a heroic message and once again shows that a person's heart has nothing to do with his house.

Narcissa Malfoy and Phineas Nigellus symbolize how much Slytherins love their families and the fact they are willing to work for the common good. Slytherins can be very emotional—in DH, for instance, we see that even Lucius Malfoy, a Slytherin Death Eater, loves Draco enough to help his son and risk the wrath of Voldemort. Harry sees that Draco is almost falling apart in HBP by being forced to make assassination attempts on Dumbledore. But since Draco has to do it to keep his parents safe, Harry's worst school rival, a Slytherin, is humanized instead of demonized.

Admittedly, it's too bad that all the Slytherin students go to safety instead of fighting at the Battle of Hogwarts, but in an interview, J.K.R. said they all came running back from Hogsmeade with help, even if it's not clear from the books. So again, she wants us to know that most of them are good, and the few twisted Slytherins are the exception. The actions of the entire house are more important than those of individual baddies like Crabbe, who tries to burn down the school or Pansy Parkinson, who stands up for Voldemort, as they did in DH. All the Slytherin kids could have run away to join Voldemort in the forest, but they never show up. It's even possible in the Epilogue that Harry's son Albus Severus might become a Slytherin. If J.K.R. leaves the door open for Harry's own son, of all people, to be a Slytherin, there's simply no way that house can be considered demonized.

Yes!

Slytherins are totally ostracized and demonized in every way throughout the books, never able to escape their image as the house of evil. Despite what J.K.R. may have said in an interview about Slytherins being "not all bad," where's the proof in the actual books? The Sorting System demonizes them, and once they are labeled rotten eggs at age eleven, they are stigmatized for the rest of their lives. Look at Snape—he was sorted at age eleven, separated from Lily, and tossed in with pureblood sociopaths. It's not his fault his housemate Mulciber was a creep, or that Lily dumped him because he wasn't sorted into Gryffindor like James Potter and Sirius Black. His life seems preordained to fail, and in due time he takes the wrong path to Death Eater-ville. Even when redeemed, Snape is still Harry's most hated teacher, and, even if the others are just as strict or demanding, Snape gets all the hateful looks and snarky answers.

Uniting just three houses is a big failure. In SS, no one listens to the Sorting Hat's song about finding "real friends" in Slytherin [SS p. 118]. We learn in the Epilogue that even when Harry's children are in school nineteen years later, they still despise and fear Slytherins. Nothing has changed. Why doesn't Harry reach out to the Slytherins when he has Dumbledore's

Army? Why doesn't Neville offer to protect the Slytherins from the Carrows? People from "worthy" houses, of course, are safe in the D.A.'s Room of Requirement, but the green and silver Slytherins are not allowed.

The scene where the Slytherins are most obviously demonized is just before the Battle of Hogwarts in DH, when Pansy Parkinson screeches out that she wants to turn Harry over to Voldemort. And why is this a surprise? Hasn't she always been a spoiled brat who hated Harry? The kids from other houses turn around and pull out their wands, as if to blast the Slytherins out of existence. Oh good, demonize and attack even the little first years because a pureblood idiot said something predictable. After that, is it any wonder that none of the Slytherins stayed to fight? Whatever J.K.R. says about their return to the battle, it's not clear at all in the book. It says that Slughorn leads relatives of people *who stayed to fight*, and that can't mean the Slytherins because none of them stayed.

From the beginning, it is drummed into us that Snape "favors" the Slytherins [SS, p. 135]. Meanwhile, in SS, McGonagall gives first year Harry a broom so he can be on her Quidditch team, and in PoA Lupin rewards the Gryffindors with loads of points for answering simple questions instead of facing their Boggarts. Dumbledore never expels or punishes Harry, no matter how many rules he breaks. In Harry's first year, Dumbledore first awards the house cup to Slytherin, then turns around and gives the Trio and Neville just enough points to win it back. It doesn't matter that the Slytherins are disappointed, since they are viewed as unworthy. Harry is the hero, so Gryffindor house is meant to win, and Slytherin "deserves" to lose because they are the bad kids who . . . aren't in Gryffindor.

And why are they all so ugly? Snape has the unfortunate grease in his hair, Narcissa has a sniffy nose problem that ruins her looks, Flint looks like a troll, and Millicent Bulstrode is fat as a toad and with the face of a hag. Is that just because Harry is so prejudiced or because they really are uglier than everyone else? It's a funny thing that other kids are seen as all right unless they are overweight like Dudley. Luna Lovegood is odd and likes to stare at people, but Harry knows right away that she is a Ravenclaw, so he never thinks that she is sinister-ugly. Demonizing Slytherins by appearance seems like the cheapest shot of all.

So where are the "good" Slytherins? Regulus Black is heroic, but only in defense of his family. In DH, he first turns Kreacher over to the Dark Lord before changing his mind, and it's not as if he wants all house-elves to go free. Also, in DH, Lucius and Narcissa want to save Draco, but only out of selfish reasons because they are protecting the last remaining Malfoy. Snape loves Lily Potter, but his love is described as a hopeless obsession with another man's wife. In J.K.R.'s 2007 Carnegie Hall interview, we learn that even the Hogwarts castle turns against Snape—in spite of the good he tries to do, he doesn't automatically get a headmaster portrait because the other portraits think he is abandoning his post. Slughorn, another Slytherin, has affection for his past students, even the Gryffindors. But he comes across as a weak social climber and, most demonizing of all, he is the one who plants the evil idea of the century—the multiple Horcruxes—in the brain of Tom Riddle. Furthermore, most of the Slytherins have nothing to do with love and family. Voldemort and Barty Crouch, Jr. admit to killing their own fathers in GoF. Bellatrix kills her cousin Sirius in OotP, and also forgets that she has a husband whenever Voldemort is around. And then there's the dysfunctional Gaunt family, with an abusive father, snake-obsessed brother, and pathetic daughter, Merope, who traps her husband with a love potion in HBP. She is also the worst mother in the entire series, giving birth to the worst villain.

The Slytherins are shown as a bunch of indoctrinated racists and cowards, who are mostly motivated by fear. Even the youngest are seen as deserving of contempt. The other houses shun them for fear they will grow up to be criminals, and no one wants to socialize with them or be their friends. Even the Slug Club, which is supposed to let the houses mingle, never results in new understanding or friendships. Harry and Ginny, the pinnacles of Gryffindor, are just as prejudiced as anybody, acting suspicious and accusatory toward any Slytherin they cross paths with, as we see in HBP when Ginny calls Blaise Zabini a "poser" in front of the Slug Club members, and then Harry follows him to his train car to spy on the Slytherin students, for instance. Yet do the books ever for a moment ask us to think that the glorified Gryffindors could possibly be wrong? No, because the demonized Slytherins are always in the wrong! A revamp of the flawed house system could have stopped the demonizing, but no one ever gets a clue about how to do that. Such a wasted opportunity for a more uplifting tale.

Verdict

Slytherins are capable of being noble, loving, and family-oriented. But that is completely overshadowed by behavior that is petty, cruel, and vindictive. The real Dark Mark of the series is that snake symbol on their robes, which is like a prophecy of doom ensuring that the other houses basically tell them to go hang and good riddance. So the verdict has to be: Yes, the Slytherins are completely and totally unfairly demonized.

Who would you rather make out with: Voldemort or a Dementor?

Voldemort

Pick Voldemort—Dementors won't just kill you, they'll suck out your soul (and we don't mean like your last boyfriend!). And who knows? You could help unlock a softer, more tender side of the Dark Lord. Maybe you could even get away with calling him "The-Man-Who-Let-The-Boy-Live" and draw a scar on his forehead in marker while he's sleeping. Plus, you won't have to worry about awkward nose collisions because, um, Voldemort *doesn't have a nose*.

His tongue is probably forked like a snake, but at least he has one, while the Dementors just have that sucker-like mouth. Kissing a Dementor would be like making out with Nemo. Ugh. At least Voldemort has teeth. Wait—does he have teeth? Fangs?

Just don't think about it. Fangs shouldn't get in the way if he has any kissing experience.

And really, he might let you keep your soul, although it will be tattered and torn, just like Bellatrix Lestrange, the Dark Lord's lady-friend. But stay out of her way, because if she catches you making out with her man, you'll be in the afterlife faster than you can say *Avada Kedavra*.

A Dementor

If you have to kiss an evil entity, go for the Dementor. It's more like kissing a potted plant with lips, and it won't last very long. That cold tingly feeling isn't love, of course, and it might bring up all your bad memories, but how is that different from say, a blind date? So just get over it. Plus, Voldemort probably has nasty B.O. and permanent morning breath. You could even say he has *killer* breath (pun very much intended). And if you hooked up with Voldemort, some people might accuse you of being a jersey chaser, because that's a guy who's going places. At least Dementors are probably good kissers because they get so much practice.

Verdict

This one's easy. If you swap spit with Voldemort, he'll probably torture and eventually kill you, but you'll still have your soul. Hooking up with a Dementor at a party would be a bigger, more eternal mistake.

What is the coolest Deathly Hallow?

The Elder Wand

Imagine the wizarding world's coolest wand choosing you as the most powerful wizard. That's what the Elder Wand does, as we learn in DH: It passes from wizard to wizard when someone is overpowered by physical force, trickery, or a spell. This is truly a case when "the wand chooses the wizard" as Mr. Ollivander explains to Harry back when he is a first-year student [SS, p. 85]. Though the Elder Wand caused treachery in the past, it doesn't really deserve the nickname "Deathstick" because the owner doesn't have to die for the magic to transfer, as Harry learns from his talk with Dumbledore in the "King's Cross" chapter. So it's cool that the Elder Wand doesn't always choose the biggest bully or killer as its master, but will respond to a wizard who uses cleverness and cunning to merely disarm an opponent, as is the case with Grindelwald, Dumbledore, Draco, and Harry.

The Elder Wand is the coolest because it sees the power in Draco and Harry that Voldemort can't see, and that they certainly can't see in themselves. The Dark Lord would never expect a powerful Hallow to view a couple of seventeen-year-old wizards as its master. Draco can't bring himself to kill Dumbledore in HBP, but he disarms him on the tower, and that is enough to impress the Elder Wand (talk about being easily impressed! Sheesh). But Draco never knows he has any special powers because the Elder Wand was buried in Dumbledore's tomb, then forcibly removed by Voldemort. When Harry later overcomes Draco and physically wrestles his own wand away, the Elder Wand wakes up and sees that as a victory, even though there is no death involved. Voldemort loves killing too much to understand the calm rationality of the Elder Wand, which can never kill Harry as long as he is the master, so Voldemort's *Avada Kedavra* backfires on him. That's a pretty cool way to win a battle against the most evil wizard the world has ever known!

The Elder Wand can be a force for good if wizards protect others with it, as Dumbledore and Harry did. It can't bring back the dead like the Resurrection Stone, and the power can't be shared as with the Invisibility Cloak, but in the hands of someone truly worthy, the Elder Wand can save the world.

The Resurrection Stone

In the Potterverse, death is all around. Harry sees dead people everywhere: headless ghosts and deathday parties, the haunting Mirror of Erised, the headmaster portraits, the Pensieve, the *Priori Incantatum* spell, the gaunt thestrals, and the voices he hears through the veil in the Department of Mysteries, for example. But Harry never truly accepts the possibility of his own death until he uses the Resurrection Stone in DH to raise the spirits of Remus Lupin, Sirius Black, and his parents, James and Lily Potter. To Harry, bringing back his loved ones is so much more important than hiding under the Cloak or using the Elder Wand because the Resurrection Stone is mystical and teaches him the spiritual lesson that death is a natural outcome of life.

The spirits of Harry's loved ones are able to talk to him, smile at him, and walk with him in the forest, explaining death to him. So his request for their presence is not selfish at all, but gives him closure on his own life so he can walk toward Voldemort bravely. He never wanted his family and friends to die for him, and now he is unafraid because he believes he will join them soon in the afterlife. All he asks in return is the knowledge of whether his own death will be painful. The answer from Sirius—that death is "easier than falling asleep"—is so simple and comforting that Harry is able to face death with courage and not waver [DH, p. 699].

And thanks to the stone, Harry is able to master death and later save other people's lives, plus he goes on to destroy Voldemort. So while the Cloak and the Elder Wand are useful tools in the fight, nothing is more important than love, which is represented by the stone. And that's always cool. Unlike the original Peverell owner, who pined away when his sweetheart returned to the grave, Harry is able to move on from grief. Mourning doesn't have to lead to sadness and depression, and death is perhaps not as final as it appears. That's a deep truth more profound than a super-wand for dueling or a magical Cloak used for child's play.

The Invisibility Cloak

Harry's Invisibility Cloak is, indeed, amusing in its possibilities. But look— it isn't just a child's toy, since it has kept the Potter family safe for hundreds of years. It is the only Deathly Hallow particularly associated with Harry's family, and it's been around since Dumbledore gave it to him for Christmas in his first year at Hogwarts. So the Cloak of Invisibility is definitely the coolest and most important of the three Hallows and the one that Harry decides to keep forever at the end of the books.

While the Resurrection Stone and the Elder Wand can be used only by their particular owners, the Cloak can be shared by anyone who needs to be protected, including the Trio in every book, the Marauders in the old days when they followed Lupin to the Shrieking Shack as described in PoA, or even Snape when he enters the Shrieking Shack to save the children. The other two Hallows cause more problems than they solve. The Resurrection Stone is all about clinging to spirits of the dead who don't want to be in the world, so why bring them back? And the Elder Wand is only for dominating or killing people—it *is* called the "Deathstick" after all. Few could resist the urge to use it for some evil purpose.

The Cloak is so much better because everyone would love to be invisible sometimes and sneak around Hogwarts, as Harry realizes from the first time he wears it. It's great for avoiding detection from Mr. Filch, although Mrs. Norris was a bit tricky, along with Mad-Eye Moody's eyeball, which could see through it. According to Dumbledore, James Potter hid under it back in the day to steal food from the Hogwarts kitchens, and, unbeknownst to Dumbledore, James had good times on the prowl as a teenage Marauder. So it's not all gloom and doom, like the other two Hallows. It's fun! As a grown-up, Harry can definitely use it in undercover work as an Auror, or just to avoid difficult or boring people—his brother-in-law Percy Weasley, perhaps? The Cloak is also great for practical jokes, such as in PoA when the cloaked Harry throws mud at Draco in Hogsmeade then terrifies him by uncovering only his own head, which eerily appears to float in midair, causing Professor Snape to sternly ask Harry later why his head was in Hogsmeade without permission. It's the cool gift that keeps on giving.

The first owner of the Cloak, Ignotus Peverell, lived a long life then died a peaceful death. Maybe turning invisible is good for a person and keeps one young at heart, which Dumbledore, with his childlike sense of humor, would certainly approve. Hopefully, Harry will enjoy the Cloak till the day when he can pass it down to his son, just in case there is some mischief to be done.

Verdict

The Elder Wand had an uncool reputation as a weapon and Harry never sought its power, yet luckily its loyalty gives him the ability to destroy Voldemort for good. However, Harry wisely puts the wand back in Dumbledore's tomb to keep it out of the hands of other bad guys in the future. The Resurrection Stone represents the awesome truth about love, death, and grief. It's awe-inspiring, but sad, which is probably why Harry drops it in the forest—so he'll never be tempted to use it again. On the other hand, it's important that he keeps the cool Invisibility Cloak handed down from the Peverells to the Potters. Harry deserves to have fun, and so do his children, who most certainly will enjoy having the power of invisibility. Verdict: The Invisibility Cloak is the coolest Hallow and probably a form of life insurance for future Potters. Plus, it totally wins the "Man, That Would be So Frickin' Sweet to Have" award.

Is the Epilogue a letdown?

Yes

For years before DH was published, J.K.R. promised that she had the last chapter of the Harry Potter series written and locked in a vault somewhere. Speculation was rampant about all the specific things that would be found in that final magical chapter about the futures of our many favorite characters. Obsessive fans wanted details about the characters, what they studied after Hogwarts, their careers and their accomplishments, so for all the buildup, the Epilogue of DH seems surprisingly vague. It is basically a happily-ever-after vision of the predictable marriages between Harry and Ginny, as well as Ron and Hermione. While most readers are glad that Harry and his friends survived to have kids, there is an emptiness in the Epilogue, with too many loose ends and not enough information. So, it is definitely a letdown.

Why did J.K.R. leave the achievements of so many characters out of the Epilogue? For instance, it's great to know that Neville becomes professor of Herbology at Hogwarts, but is that more important than finding out what Harry himself does for a living? The career paths of the main characters are not mentioned at all, which is disappointing when education and magical studies are so much the focus of the series. J.K.R. had all the answers in her post-DH interviews, such as her Bloomsbury Live Chat in which she revealed that Harry and Ron become Aurors working with Kingsley Shacklebolt, Hermione becomes an attorney for the Ministry of Magic, and Ginny plays professional Quidditch for the Holyhead Harpies. It's a big letdown that the author would choose to leave out those sharp personal details on purpose, then go on television and talk about what wasn't in the Epilogue just a few days after the book release. It left fans shaking their heads because they wanted answers on the written page and a definitive conclusion, and it just isn't there in the Epilogue.

Another big subject left completely out of the Epilogue is whether or not there have been reforms in the wizarding world since Voldemort died. The books gave us the idea that Harry's generation could overthrow the old ways and make a difference to society. Yet years after the dust has settled from the last battle, nothing seems to have changed. Nineteen years later, Hogwarts still has the rusty old Sorting System, with Ron joking that he will disown his kids if they aren't in Gryffindor. Draco Malfoy, who is also seen in the Epilogue putting his child on the train for Hogwarts, probably told his son Scorpius the same thing about choosing Slytherin over Gryffindor, so the prejudices continue to a new generation. To his credit, Harry tells his son Albus Severus that house rivalries don't matter, but he also undercuts that advice by telling the child how to beat the system and ask the Sorting Hat to put him in Gryffindor. So the Slytherin stigma continues, and the houses are still not unified.

Not only are the fates of the vast majority of characters missing in the Epilogue, there are also no clues about the fate of house-elves, goblins, or werewolves. What happened to S.P.E.W., the Society for Preservation of Elfish Welfare, started by Hermione? Were goblins ever treated fairly by wizards and allowed to carry wands? Were werewolves ever given basic human rights such as being able to hold jobs? These questions were raised many times in the series, and even in the W.O.M.B.A.T. tests given on the official site. But we don't get any answers in the Epilogue.

What we do see in the DH Epilogue are some of the children of the main characters, yet the fans could scarcely believe some of the names. Draco's child Scorpius seems to have a dark Death Eater name, though Draco supposedly reformed. In contrast, the names of Ron and Hermione's kids, Rose and Hugo, seem to have been chosen just because they match the initials of their parents. Harry's three children are each named for people significant to him alone, with the oldest named James for Harry's father and the youngest named Lily for Harry's mother. The middle Potter child is named for Dumbledore and Severus Snape, the ever-sarcastic professor who never had a kind word to say to Harry. That just seems beyond belief and surprising in a bad way. And it begs the question of why Ginny would be so compliant on the names when she was always so opinionated and feisty throughout the series. She has certainly toned herself down a lot because not one of her children is named after anyone in the Weasley family, not even Ginny's father, Arthur, or her favorite brother, Bill, or her dead brother, Fred. Yes, we see Bill and Fleur's daughter, Victoire, who is snogging Lupin's son Teddy, but where are George Weasley's children? Or Percy's, since Harry overhears him talking in the train station? Why set the Epilogue in King's Cross and miss a golden opportunity to show us the children of many more characters as they gathered to catch the Hogwarts Express? We wanted so much more!

No

The Epilogue is not a letdown, unless readers had unrealistic expectations. J.K.R. could never write enough backstory to please all of her readers, and it would have been impossible to pack every detail about the characters into the last chapter. Who would want the series to end with a big genealogy chart? So J.K.R. had to focus on the most important characters that have been at the heart of the story from the beginning—Harry, Ron, and Hermione—and their children. If the chapter has a fairy-tale quality to it, it is because the characters have suffered and deserve a peaceful future. That's the emotional payoff. And who cares if every detail is not explored? The author told an interviewer on NBC's *Today Show* just after DH was released that she was going for a "nebulous" quality that didn't give everything away [JKR-TD]. Every great book leaves something to the readers' imaginations, and that is also true of *Deathly Hallows*. Additionally, we know J.K.R. is in the process of compiling an encyclopedia full of niggling details to satiate her most rabid fans.

Plenty of story lines are completed by the Epilogue. Harry has the family he always wanted. The orphaned Teddy Lupin has been accepted as a family member by Harry and Ginny. Harry's children are the namesakes of those who tried to save Harry, and he and Draco seem to respect each other as adults. And the next generation of children is on their way to Hogwarts to begin their magical education and to complete the circle started by Book One.

If the emphasis is not on career, education, fame, or glory, perhaps that's the point the author is trying to make. Love and family are more important than any career goal. After all, Harry's vision of the afterlife was the warmth and calm of King's Cross, and that is where he is in the Epilogue. He has his heaven on earth. Whatever his work as an adult has been, it could never be as rewarding as those moments with his children, so it's not necessary to explain his job description, or Hermione's, or Ron's. Neville is mentioned because he is a survivor, too, and though he doesn't have children yet, he is still involved in the next generation as a teacher. It's all about the kids.

In an Epilogue, which has the theme of hope and well-being in the future, stories about government reform would be heavy-handed and out of place. Nothing can change overnight, and some of the traditions of the wizarding world go back centuries. S.P.E.W. was a good idea, but Hermione never managed to convert any house-elves with her idealism. Prejudice in society against werewolves and goblins, as well as students in Slytherin house, could not possibly change overnight. The death of Voldemort did not create a perfect society, nor did the death of Dumbledore mean that Hogwarts would completely change the system. The children going off to Hogwarts symbolize the system being changed from within and the good things that can happen in the future.

The final chapter had to balance the darkness in the rest of the book and the series as a whole. After Voldemort's reign of torture and terror, who wouldn't want nineteen years of peace and quiet? Harry's grown up, he's having a good life, and things have come full circle for his family. That's not a letdown, it's a victory.

Verdict

The Epilogue is sadly not what many readers envisioned in their Mirror of Erised or desire. In a series with hundreds of characters, we learn the fates of only a few. At the end of a long dark tunnel, there is too much sweetness and light, without any shadows except that the wizarding world is stuck with the prejudices of the past. Of course, other readers love the glowing emphasis on family life and children, but what else have Harry and his friends accomplished in nineteen years? New details that trickle out from J.K.R.'s interviews are fun to know, but it would have been so much better for the readers if the Epilogue gave us the scoop at least about the main characters. Verdict: The Epilogue is an unfortunate letdown.

Would you rather shave Hagrid's back or give Voldemort a foot massage?

Give Voldemort a Foot Massage

Voldemort didn't have any feet for quite a few years when he was an unembodied soul, so once he had a body again, a foot massage might be just the ticket to put him in a relaxing, snakelike trance. And while he's in a good mood, he's not out torturing humanity for a while, so it's like doing a public service. Yes, it's true that if you tickle him or break a blister, he is going to *Crucio* you. But afterward, you won't be covered with mounds of coarse black hair and whatever else might fall out of Hagrid's back fur. And Voldie's feet are surely much smaller than Hagrid's massive shoulders, so the foot massage has to be less time-consuming. Foot odor? That is nothing compared to whatever might arise if Hagrid had Taco Bell for dinner.

Shave Hagrid's Back

Get real—each one of Voldemort's toenails are probably as sharp as ninja swords and you'll lose all your fingers. And for fun, he'll use you as a footstool and probably kick a dark mark into your forehead.

With Hagrid's back hair, it's true you might need a small lawnmower to do the job correctly, and there will be enough hair leftover to weave a couple of rugs. But you know he'll be so grateful. The gentle giant will make you a big cup of tea and offer you a rock cake. Then you can pet the fuzzy critters in his hut (avoiding the Skrewts), and ask his advice about all your problems (though we don't know why you'd ever do this). That's much more pleasant than a brain concussion, claw marks, and reptilian foot odor any day.

Verdict

No matter how you grovel at the feet of the Dark Lord and no matter how magical your fingers are, Voldemort will never thank you for a foot massage. However, if you do Hagrid the small favor of trimming his back bush, he will be your friend for life. Verdict: Please bring your hedge clippers to Hagrid's hut.

Which character fails to live up to expectations?

Remus Lupin

Professor Remus Lupin starts out in PoA as one of the best characters, the disabled underdog in society who can't get a break but stays calm and hopeful. Showing up at Hogwarts carrying a beat-up suitcase and wearing a shabby suit, he becomes Harry's favorite teacher, a mentor, and Harry soon finds out that Lupin is an old friend of the family. He's also a werewolf, which instantly makes him super cool. But once he loses his job as a popular professor at Hogwarts, he never gets back on track for the rest of the series. Lupin just isn't there for Harry most of the time, and he often seems preoccupied with his own problems.

Lupin drops out of Harry's life for all of GoF, and shows up again in OotP as an Order of the Phoenix member, but his main function for the rest of that book is to babysit his old friend Sirius Black. There isn't much new character development and he mostly just hangs around Grimmauld Place eating and drinking and talking, until he is needed in the fight at the Ministry. He shows up at Christmas in HBP, telling Harry that he works as a secret agent for Dumbledore among the werewolves, but what does he actually do? No one knows. As readers, we want to picture the "werewolf underground" with secret meetings and Lupin making deals as a spy, but that never materializes in the books. He could have been the coolest literary werewolf of all time, but we only see him transform one time at the end of PoA, and after that he seems to lose the power of the inner beast.

Then there's Lupin's love life, which is a disaster. The young witch Nymphadora Tonks falls in love with him beginning in OotP and continues to moon over him through HBP, and Lupin can't seem to decide how he feels about her. If he really loved Nymphadora Tonks at all, why did Mr. and Mrs. Weasley have to talk him into marrying her? Is it just because he fears that he is too old for her? Or is there just a lack of passion on his part, which is the way it seems from his underwhelming response to her? It's obvious that married life didn't agree with him because as soon as he discovers that his wife is pregnant in DH, Lupin hits the road, making the juvenile decision to run away with the teenagers on their quest for the Horcruxes and Hallows. It's a cringe-worthy Marauder midlife crisis in the middle of a war, and it's a disappointment to fans who thought Lupin was a loyal, stand-up guy. Only an intervention from suddenly mature Harry calling him cowardly keeps Lupin from being a deadbeat dad, and to his credit, he goes back home to Tonks. But, by then, readers have lost all respect for him, and when Lupin turns up later at Shell Cottage handing out cigars as the proud papa, even Harry, who agrees to be godfather to Lupin's son, can't seem to believe it.

Lupin has a few great moments in the books—he teaches Harry the Expecto Patronum Charm in PoA; he's awesome as the leader of the Advance Guard in OotP; and he saves Harry from following Sirius Black through the Death Veil. But how great it could have been in DH if we had seen Lupin having a smack-down duel with Fenrir Greyback, the werewolf who bit him as a child? Instead, Lupin is written in such a deadly dull way that he might have tried to just reasonably talk Greyback into a coma. While it's true that Lupin steps up to fight at the Battle of Hogwarts, we don't see him fight, and we miss the death scene, so it lacks that meaningful blaze of glory. The last time we see him in DH is when Harry calls him back from the dead with the Resurrection Stone, and his spirit makes a gooey speech about wanting to save the world for his son. Sorry, Professor, your life story just isn't the inspirational beauty-and-the-beast tale that the author tries to sell us.

Nymphadora Tonks

If Lupin's life story failed to live up to expectations, maybe it was because he married another sadly unexceptional character: Nymphadora Tonks. Of all the female characters, she turns out to be the most tiresome girl in the series. That is a shame, considering how cute she is when we first see her in OotP. She is this young, snappy, streetwise Auror with purple hair, joking around with crusty Mad-Eye Moody. Yet, unfortunately over the next two books, Tonks's life collapses into a sort of manic-depressive hair commercial, with mood swings out of a psychology textbook, and it's all about her ill-fated romance with Remus Lupin. She falls apart when he can't go on moonlit strolls with her and won't marry her, and that interferes with her job performance as a guard stationed at Hogwarts. Why can't she pull herself together? Eventually, when Lupin succumbs to pressure from the Weasleys and marries her in DH, Tonks dumps her career apparently to stay at home and be a mom. Funny—that's when Lupin completely loses interest in her and tries to run away from home. It wouldn't have surprised anyone if they had gone to a werewolf marriage counselor.

Tonks is a Metamorphmagus, able to change her appearance at will without potions or spells, which makes her almost a superhero, and her many disguises are so exciting that the possibilities are endless for a story set in wartime. *She* should have been the spy—not Remus. So it falls short of expectations that all she does is guard Harry in HBP, standing around in Hogsmeade and patrolling Hogwarts. Yawn. Anyone could have herded Harry around, and she doesn't really act like a cool Auror anymore. Nymphadora is so sick with puppy love that she overlooks the plot of her cousin Draco to let Death Eaters into the school. What good is an Auror who can't do detective work?

At first, Tonks is vivacious, delightful, and full of energy. But love saps all that out of her. Lupin may lose the inner beast, but Tonks loses her identity as a tough, independent girl. Her hair turns from passionate pink to mousy brown—horrors—and then her Patronus changes into a galloping werewolf. At first it seems unfair when Snape tells her the Patronus makes her seem weak, but in hindsight, he is right. Her character becomes as washed-out as her hair, and she never lives up to more colorful expectations.

Verdict

Tonks, we barely knew ye, but most of the time, you remind us of the sad and pathetic phases in our lives after we got dumped by our exes. And those weren't happy times. Lupin, you could have been a contender for alpha male, but instead you end up like a washed-up star. Verdict: Both of them fall far short of expectations, but Lupin has more page-time than Tonks. Sorry, Lupin, we expected so much more from you.

Would you want to be a wizard if it meant giving up all your friends?

No!

It's neither better nor worse to be magical—both worlds have their own problems. But how could it be right to give up all your Muggle friends and throw away everything you had built up in your old life? No one should ever throw away relationships just to play around with magic. That goes completely against the message of the books, which is that friendship is the most important thing in life.

Being magical would also mean learning to deal with new dangers, such as Blast-Ended Skrewts, Dementors, and werewolves. Ordinary activities can also be painful: You might crash into a helicopter while flying on a broom, or splinch while Apparating somewhere. You might not get cancer or heart disease, but wizards still break out in Dragon Pox or Spattergroit. If you are ill and have to go to St. Mungos Hospital for Magical Maladies and Injuries, some of the cures are worse than the diseases. Ugh—Skelegrow!

And look at all the things you'd be giving up. Since magic interferes with electricity, there would be no more iPods, laptops, or 15 megapixel digital cameras. Forget instant messaging—you'd be sending all your messages by owl, and that takes days for a reply, essentially turning the clock back one hundred years on Muggle technology. And a Pensieve is no replacement for YouTube.

You'd be trapped in a society where people sit around mending brooms, reading books (who does that?), and dressing like monks from the Middle Ages (come on, jeans are way more comfortable than robes). Quidditch is lacrosse on broomsticks, which sounds awesome, but the Snitch is worth so many points that most of the action is completely pointless. The game is ultimately a glorified Easter Egg hunt. It is so unclear what wizards do for entertainment, besides the wireless radio with really bad songs or rock bands, like the Weird Sisters. There may be nightclubs and music, but are there plays or movies? Is there a wizarding Broadway? Is there a magical equivalent to the DVD? Without answers to those questions, it could be a long and lonely banishment into magical limbo with nothing to do, and no friends to hang out with. No wonder Sirius Black was bored all the time.

Yes!

This is a no-brainer since you should be glad to let go of your boring Muggle friends and enter the enchanted alternate universe. You'll make new wizarding friends anyway, and pretty soon you won't have much in common with the old crowd, as you learn to Apparate, fly on a broom, and use the Floo Network. Additionally, it is important for the witches and wizards from non-wizarding families to intermix with magical people to provide diversity to the world and be a de facto source of vicarious Muggle participation.

So what if you give up computers and television? You can frickin' *fly*. The sky's *not even* the limit. There are a million reasons why choosing between being a wizard and being a Muggle is a no-brainer. Here are a few: *Accio* (this one should need no explanation), *Expelliarmus* (for protection against ninjas), *Protego* (again, for ninja protection), *Engorgio* (um...), *Reparo* (now, if this only worked for relationships!), *Scourgio* ("sure, I'll do the dishes!"), *Silencio* (for that girl on the bus who talks so loud you can hear her even with Fall Out Boy blasting through your iPod's noise-cancelling earbuds). But, really, you only need one reason, and here it is: Apparation. *Booyah!* And with magic to help you through life, you'll have free time to travel and relax on a beach somewhere, with a house-elf to mix tropical drinks. Let your old friends go to the mall and shop while you go to Diagon Alley for a bunch of Weasley's Wizard Wheezes and a new Firebolt. It will be like the best movie you ever saw, and you will be the hero. You'll be a giant ball of awesomeness superior to the combined awesomeness of all six billion Muggles on earth. Once you find your magical talent, whether it is Potions, Herbology, Defense Against the Dark Arts, or Care of Magical Creatures, you won't miss anyone. Except Oprah. What a sweetie.

Verdict

It's tempting to run away and join the wizarding world, leaving the dull life of Muggledom behind. Your friends will think you've just changed schools or found a new job, and meanwhile you'll be conjuring up the time of your life. However, magic can't buy you better companions, as Peter Pettigrew found out. Psychology has taught us that happiness is more closely related to emotional health and tends not to increase as one accumulates material possessions. And if you decimated all of your relationships to go start a new life, it would be for the wrong reasons. Even wizards get lonely, so don't give up your friends. That is, unless your Muggle life completely sucks and you have no friends. In that case, what have you got to lose? Verdict: Ultimately, it's a personal decision.

What is the cheesiest movie moment?

The Bathtub Scene with Myrtle (GoF)

The cheese-fest actually starts when Cedric Diggory looks all around and then whispers to Harry that he should take his egg to the Prefect's bathroom for a nice soak in the tub. It sounds so bizarre. Can you imagine what moviegoers who haven't read the books must think about that? Because then we see semi-naked Harry slide into a bathtub the size of small swimming pool, while a mermaid peeks at him from the stained-glass window. Ewww—the kid is supposed to be fourteen years old. If that isn't reason enough for viewers to fast-forward, or at least do a facepalm, in floats Moaning Myrtle, the most annoying ghost in the world. From her yucking and overdone ghost giggling to the fact that she is leering at Harry through the bubbles, it's a smorgasbord of assorted cheese.

And then there is the whole-yolk reason for the scene: the Golden Egg. Earlier when Harry opened it in the Gryffindor Common Room, it shrieked loudly. (That scene was actually a runner-up for this category because Harry grins broadly and says, "Who wants me to open it? Do you want me to open it?" It's like a cheese and corn omelette.) But getting back to the bathroom, Myrtle gets closer and closer to naked Harry—ewww again—until she tells him the "other boy" put the egg under the water. (Great—she's been slithering around the tub with Cedric, too.) But under the soapsuds we go, while Myrtle waves her hands around the precious egg, which is a tacky movie prop that looks like a round lava lamp full of hair gel. And lo, it opens and starts to sing the clear mermaid song, but no one ever listens because they quickly hit the "stop" button or fast-forward to the death of Cedric. Viewers who actually watch that scene need a shower afterward to rinse away the cheese residue.

The Return of Hermione and Hagrid (CoS)

Well, at least Myrtle in the bathtub with the egg is "supposed" to be funny—that's what all the giggling is about. But there's another scene that is totally cheesy because it's meant to be sweet and inspirational, but turns out all goofy and pointless. That's the scene called "Welcome Back" at the end of CoS. For a scene that goes on and on, it has a simple theme—everyone comes back—surprise! Hermione gets sprung from the hospital wing where she's been Petrified, and Hagrid comes back from Azkaban. It should take all of three minutes, but it's more like being trapped in an extra-cheese calzone for three weeks.

This is the scene that gave us a big "shipping" clue about the future love interest of Hermione. She runs with leaps and bounds (thankfully not in slow-motion) into the platonic arms of huggable Harry, but then gets all flustered and shy over nearly mute and stuttering Ron. The lack of talking and physical contact of any kind was a clear sign that Hermione and Ron were meant to be together. But it was not totally and completely obvious. Ahem. This reunion is dripping with cheddary goodness, but the "big" helping of gooey mozzarella is still to come.

After Dumbledore makes a speech—Yay for the Mandrake Potion and exams being canceled—the fondue separates . . . no . . . the door opens, and in walks the big guy, Rubeus Hagrid. Now forget the fact that no one has thought about Hagrid at all for the past few scenes because Hermione hasn't been there to remind them. Forget the fact that most viewers haven't even noticed he was gone. He has got to be welcomed with hoopla and hoop cheese, hugs, and frozen grins. Eventually, the cheesiest line in the whole entire series is spoken, with Harry staring at Hagrid like a basilisk. No, a cheese-laden owl: "It's not Hogwarts without you, Hagrid."

The rest of it is probably written in the script this way: smile, smile, hug. Dumbledore claps so slowly you might think his hand is Horcruxed already, McGonagall smiles, Hagrid smiles, Harry claps, then grins with extra Parmesan sprinkled on top. (Is it over yet? No, you clown!) Hufflepuffs clap as if they can't get their hands to meet together. Slytherins clap—but only the nameless "good" ones, as unsmiling Draco forces Crabbe to sit down. (Why is that bad? No one knows what they are clapping for anyway.)

Then every child in the room gets up suddenly and runs toward Hagrid for some inexplicable reason, and the group hugs and handshakes go on for another ten minutes until it all starts to smell like aging Limberger. (They left out scenes from the book to make time for this?) Finally, the Trio smiles, Hagrid smiles, Dumbledore smiles because he's clearly lost track of what's going on, all the teachers say "cheese" (except Alan Rickman of course, who is still wondering why Pomfrey and Sprout got credit for Snape's Mandrake Draught and stole another scene from him), and finally the cameraman flies right out the window because he just can't take it anymore.

The Freeze-Frame Ending (PoA)

The third movie is considered by many to be the best movie produced so far. However, its ending was atrocious. The freeze frame the producers chose before rolling the credits was a snapshot of Harry's face in a wide-open tree-frog laugh. It was so hilariously awkward that the MuggleNet switchboards exploded with fan reports from all around the world confirming that theater audiences actually erupted with laughter at the ridiculousness of it. Oh, Hollywood.

"He Was Their Friend!" (PoA)

When Harry goes to Hogsmeade and overhears Fudge and McGonagall saying that Sirius Black was the one who betrayed his family, it's more than he can handle. Hermione and Ron later find him sobbing in the snow under the Invisibility Cloak. As the camera zooms in on his emo face, Harry shrieks, "He was their friend... And he betrayed them. HE WAS THEIR FRIEND!! I hope he finds me. Cause when he does, I'm gonna be ready! When he does, I'm gonna kill him!" Unfortunately, then the camera lingers on Dan's angry clenched teeth. Cringe.

Verdict

Moaning Myrtle's hiccupping laugh in GoF sounds like someone choking to death on a Subway $5 footlong, and you just wish you could pull out a gun and kill her again. Dan Radcliffe is blushing with embarrassment not because he is butt-naked in a bathtub, but because he's talking to a plastic egg. The ending of CoS, by contrast, has every illustrious actor in the movie doing the same thing—smiling until their faces show the pain. The basilisk could not Petrify viewers quicker than this cringe-worthy scene, which most fans never finish watching because it puts them into a cheesecake coma. It's the kind of scene you hope no one walks in on you watching, lest they embarrass you like your parents did when a kissing scene came on. Verdict: The endless Hermione/Hagrid hug-a-thon is definitely the cheesiest movie scene.

Who (besides Voldemort) is the character you hate the most?

Vernon Dursley

It's hard to think of a character in the series more hateful than Harry's uncle, Vernon Dursley, who really gives Muggles a bad name. Mean and spiteful even when Harry is just a baby, Vernon lets Petunia adopt Harry but never really treats him like a member of the family. He's a horrible father figure, as we see in SS, keeping Harry locked in a closet under the stairs, making him wear hand-me-downs, forcing him to do most of the housework, and almost refusing the admission letters sent by Hogwarts. Although he knows that magic is real and believes that Petunia's sister Lily was a witch, he's in major denial and is unwilling to accept Harry's special gifts. He makes sure the neighbors on Privet Drive believe that Harry is a problem child from St. Brutus's Secure Center for Incurably Criminal Boys, which he also tells his similar loudmouth sister, Aunt Marge, in PoA. He's an absolute total scumbag.

Vernon's worst trait is the physical abuse he heaps on Harry, as we see in OotP when he turns purple while trying to strangle him just for eavesdropping outside a window. Vernon is definitely just as threatening to the boy's life as Voldemort ever was. He also encourages his juvenile delinquent son, Dudley, to both physically and verbally abuse Harry. Magic is probably the only thing keeping Harry alive sometimes, with this tag team of goons at home. Sadly, Petunia goes along with Vernon on everything, favoring her Popkin while starving Harry for both food and affection. But at least when Vern tries to toss Harry out on the street after a Dementor attacks Dudley in OotP, Petunia has the courage to stand up to her husband and tell him that Harry has to remain in their home. Who knows? Maybe Petunia would have been a better aunt all along if Vernon didn't have the mentality of a tubeworm and the personality of an angry walrus.

Cornelius Fudge

While Vernon Dursley is just a petty dictator in his own home, the character Cornelius Fudge causes trouble for the whole world, and Harry in particular, so in some ways he's nearly as bad as Voldemort. He's the freakin' Minister of Magic, with an Auror police squad at his beck and call, but Fudge can't seem to protect Harry from danger. Talk about denial—after Voldemort rises again in GoF, Cornelius refuses to believe it, so in OotP he encourages the *Daily Prophet* to smear both Dumbledore and Harry as mentally disturbed liars. Fudge is almost worse than Vernon because he takes away the one refuge Harry has left, which is the magical world. In OotP, he also installs his protégé, the hideous Professor Dolores Umbridge, as the High Inquisitor at Hogwarts, and school becomes a misery, not just for Harry, but for all the students and teachers. Vernon at least looks out for his own family of Petunia and Dudley, but old Corny Fudge doesn't care about anyone or anything except his own reputation as Minister of Magic.

Fudge is a smarmy politician who reminds us of an awful lot of Muggle politicians. He likes to be seen as caring toward The Boy Who Lived, but tosses Harry aside when public opinion turns. Fudge favors the wealthy and racist purebloods, so he's an even worse snob than the middle-class Vernon, who at least works for a living. All Fudge really wants is to hang on to power and control, and he doesn't really know how to run the government with any success unless Dumbledore helps him. So where brains are concerned, Cornelius Fudge and Vernon Dursley are just about equally stupid.

Professor Dolores Umbridge

To even entertain the possibility of a more insufferable character is an insult to Dolores Umbridge herself. Umbridge is actually a Ministry of Magic official installed at Hogwarts by Cornelius Fudge to interfere and spy on Dumbledore. Her mantra is "wands away" while the kids sit reading a boring textbook, and she punishes them for talking back or doing any minor offense [OotP, p. 239]. Her black quill of pain is an instrument of torture worthy of Voldemort. As if writing lines in blood isn't enough, Umbridge also unethically tries to dose Harry's tea with the truth-telling potion Veritaserum to get information for the Ministry about Dumbledore's plans. She truly loves her job, but expanding and educating young minds is not the point, and she is more of a jail warden than a teacher.

As bad people go, the block-headed and evil Carrows in DH probably inflicted more pain on the schoolchildren, but Umbridge is more subtle and scary, with her little girl voice and her kitty cat plates on the wall. And who can forget her hideous "hem-hem" giggle that drove everyone crazy? She's the devil in a pink cardigan.

It's true that Snape is just as blunt and insulting to students who don't make the grade, such as poor Neville, who burns cauldrons into puddles of metallic goop. But Snape actually teaches his students, and when he gives detentions, they are all very humdrum Muggle-style tasks, such as scrubbing bedpans without magic, writing an extra essay, or copying notecards from Filch's filing cabinet. He never carves up a student's hand for fun and amusement. Snape is obviously working against Umbridge, refusing to give her unlimited Veritaserum and lying to Draco about Harry's Occlumency lessons so Umbridge won't find out.

In fact, all the teachers hate Umbridge with a passion, and she drives them completely insane with her evaluations. She is sarcastic and rude, and she interrupts classes constantly in a year when the students need to study for O.W.L. exams. She does her best to destroy the teaching staff, throwing Madam Trelawney down the stairs and nearly out of the school, helping Fudge and his Aurors attack Dumbledore, fighting against Hagrid and chasing him from the grounds, and Stunning elderly Professor McGonagall, which sends her to the hospital. Is all that in the name of education?

It's too bad that the centaurs don't finish off Umbridge when they carry her away at the end of OotP. And it's too bad it isn't the end for her when Peeves the Poltergeist chases her out the door of the school while hitting her with a bag of chalk. Unfortunately, she turns up again at the Ministry in DH, torturing Muggle-borns and throwing them in prison. She even uses the late Mad-Eye Moody's magical eyeball as a security system on her office door—how sick is that? Is it any surprise that she enjoys wearing Salazar Slytherin's locket, which was one of Voldemort's Horcruxes? It probably feels completely normal to her, since her mind is already twisted. Harry should have kept her around as a natural Patronus Charm—Dementors wouldn't touch (or kiss) that soulless creature with a thirty-nine-and-a-half-foot pole. You want to murder her, but that's not enough—you want to clone her and kill all her clones.

Verdict

As a leader, Cornelius Fudge could have helped Harry by hunting down the Dark Lord when he was still a pre-cauldron speck of a soul, but he let tunnel vision and lack of action nearly destroy the wizarding world. Vernon Dursley could have been a real dad to Harry, but he withheld fatherly love and affection. Verdict: When it all comes down, Dolores Umbridge is the character whose head you most want to hold underwater.

Who is the better supporting character: Luna Lovegood or Neville Longbottom?

Luna Lovegood

What makes Luna Lovegood the best supporting character by far is that although she seems lost in a whimsical world of her own, she manages to have a special friendship with Harry that goes beyond houses, gender, or popularity. She is an outcast when we first see her sitting alone on the train in OotP, but soon everyone comes to appreciate her piercing insights and total honesty. She is sweet and funny, making Harry laugh with her more bizarre tales of the Rotfang Conspiracy and the Crumple-Horned Snorkack. In some ways, she's the best role model for girls in the books because she always does her own thing without caring what anyone thinks.

She helps Harry learn to have faith in the unseen parts of the universe. No one else can explain the veil in the Death Room or the haunting Thestrals. Luna doesn't try to explain everything logically, as Hermione does, and she also doesn't fall apart and cry when she is sad, like Cho Chang. She is also Ginny Weasley's friend, as she mentions in HBP when commentating hilariously for the Quidditch match, but she doesn't have the same flaring temper even when the bullies are bothering her. In some ways, Luna is a combination of all the houses, except Slytherin. Although she definitely supports her own Ravenclaw house at Quidditch, even letting their mascot—a large eagle—perch on her head in OotP, she also wears a roaring lion hat and likes to sit with the courageous Gryffindors. She is loyal and true like a Hufflepuff, but doesn't seem to have a Slytherin bone in her body.

Luna isn't afraid of the unknown, while nervous Neville often worries about everything. Luna's like a mystical princess who is always calm and cool, even in DH when she's been kidnapped and tortured at Malfoy Manor, or when she is standing by Dobby's grave giving his eulogy. Luna is a calm spirit, a breath of fresh air, and a comfort to everyone. Plus, she's hilarious. How empty the books would be without her!

Neville Longbottom

Luna is a great girl, but did she ever destroy a Horcrux? No. Did she ever talk back to Voldemort or lead Dumbledore's Army? No. And that's why the best supporting character has to be Neville Longbottom. He was nearly the "Chosen One" himself, born just one day before Harry on June 30, according to J.K.R.'s official site. Throughout the story he is just one step behind. He has so much in common with Harry that they are almost like brothers.

While Luna still has her father, Neville and Harry are both orphans raised by other relatives. Neville's grandmother cares about him, but she's also strict and fussy, expecting him to fall short of his own parents. Frank Longbottom was an Auror at one time, but was later rendered insane by Death Eaters along with his wife Alice, whom we see in a poignant scene with Neville at St. Mungo's Hospital in OotP. So Neville is a survivor and has a lot to overcome as he grows up, from facing his scary Boggart, Professor Snape the Potions Master in PoA, to fighting the evil Bellatrix Lestrange, torturer of his parents, in OotP. He also isn't afraid to cross his own friends as we first see in SS when Neville tries to stop the Trio from sneaking around and losing points (which later helps Gryffindor win the house cup). In DH, Neville could have played it safe and used his pureblood status as protection since Voldemort wants to preserve the purest wizards while killing off those with what he thinks is tainted blood. Instead, Neville stands up to the Death Eater Carrows who torture him, he keeps Dumbledore's Army going, and he tells Voldemort that hell will freeze over before he will become a Death Eater.

Neville is like a brave knight of old who doesn't know if he can win all his battles but keeps trying anyway. With his kind nature and love of plants, he could have been a Hufflepuff all the way, yet in DH he has his finest moment when he pulls the Sword of Gryffindor out of the Sorting Hat to slay Voldemort's giant serpent Horcrux Nagini. The books are Neville's hero tale as much as Harry's, and perhaps his story is even more important because he had to do things on his own and find his own style of courage without help.

Verdict

Luna Lovegood is not afraid to be herself and she teaches Harry to look beyond appearances. Neville has a different role—he has to live in Harry's shadow, but follow his own path to greatness. And in the end, Harry trusts Neville to keep up the fight and do the right thing. Both of these characters are crucial to Harry's success, but the verdict is: Neville is the one who plays the best supporting role.

Which duel is the best in the series?

Harry and Voldemort in the Graveyard (GoF)

Most of the duels in HP are over within the blink of an eye, but the grave-yard duel in GoF is lengthy and action-packed, so it is the best of the series. It occurs after Harry and Cedric Diggory have been tricked into using the Triwizard Tournament Cup as a Portkey, which takes them into the clutches of Peter Pettigrew and Lord Voldemort in the graveyard where Tom Riddle's father is buried. Not only does Harry see his friend Cedric killed in cold blood, Harry is then tied to a headstone, traumatized, bleeding and men-tally calling out for the police. He doesn't seem to stand a chance against the newly arisen Voldemort. And, of course, the Noseless One has to laugh at the poor kid, taunting him about his dead parents, and he forces Harry to bow against his will, making a farce of the rules of dueling learned in CoS. Voldemort also cheats by knocking Harry down with a painful *Crucio* first, while the Death Eaters stand around and chuckle. But from the minute the real dueling action begins, the grins are wiped from their sadistic faces.

How great to see the usually boring *Expelliarmus* spell, which makes wands fly from someone's hand, become something truly magical. It is the only spell Harry knows for dueling at this point in the series, and he just wants to knock Voldemort's wand away and make a run for the Portkey so he can get back to Hogwarts. Instead, something amazing happens when Harry's wand connects with Voldemort's: He and the Dark Lord are lifted up like floating cage fighters in a dome of bright light. Harry begins to hear music that reminds him of the song of the phoenix, always a hopeful sound, and that seems to cause Voldemort to freak out as he is clueless about what is happening. To the surprise of the Death Eater crowd, their fearless leader is at the mercy of his own wand, which connects with Harry's because they both have phoenix feathers inside them (as explained by Mr. Ollivander in SS). No other duel in the series has this *Priori Incantatum* effect, and it's awe-inspiring when Voldemort's murder victims start popping out of his evil wand to protect Harry. Even Harry's dead parents appear and give him advice for how to escape, while Voldemort is left literally hanging at the end of the fiery rope of light. Harry has no plan for revenge in this duel—he just wants to go the distance and stay alive. But Harry wins on points because Voldemort's bad actions come back from the past to bite him. Even when the song of the phoenix dies and the light goes out, the spirits of the dead still act as human shields so that Harry can run away. Nobody dies or even gets hurt, and the return of the spirits is all foreshadowing for the Resurrection Stone scene in DH when Harry's parents come back to walk with him to his death.

The satisfaction of the duel is that Voldemort goes through the range of emotions, from arrogance and disdain to fear and absolute shock, and then furious outrage. He is totally shaken up and blown away, which is the point of the duel. Harry beats the odds and beats the old man at his game. It's the longest, the best, and the most dramatic of all the dueling scenes in the books.

Dumbledore and Voldemort at the Ministry (OotP)

Because Albus Dumbledore was the "only one he ever feared," Voldemort has never dueled with him until they come face-to-face at the Ministry of Magic in OotP [p. 813]. What the Dark Lord didn't know then, nor did the readers, is that Dumbledore had a secret weapon—the Deathly Hallow known as the Elder Wand, which was considered unbeatable. And in this duel, it's clear that for an old guy, Dumbledore still has the right stuff to take down Voldemort. He spins and twirls while casting jinxes and dodging Unforgiveable Curses, and at the same time brings the large golden Ministry statues to life so they can protect Harry. Dumbledore acts "as though he had not a fear in the world" and lectures the Dark Lord on life and death "as if he was discussing it over drinks" [p. 814]. How cool is that? Fawkes the phoenix shows up to swallow a green burst of the killing spell *Avada Kedavra*, but Dumbledore never tries to kill his old student Tom Riddle in return: He just wants to capture him and lock him up, which is the same way he overcame his old friend, Gellert Grindelwald back in 1945. But Voldemort is too slippery and tries to possess Harry before the boy's pure soul power drives Voldemort away. He is last seen carrying off Bellatrix Lestrange and

Disapparating, so Dumbledore puts Voldemort on the run. Voldemort has truly met his match in his old professor. A duel between Voldemort and Dumbledore—two of the biggest badasses in wizarding history—has to be the most epic duel ever, by default.

Molly and Bellatrix at Hogwarts (DH)

Harry duels Voldemort over and over and everyone knows who has to win, so it's a big yawn. The best duel is the one that is totally unexpected, coming out of nowhere at the Battle of Hogwarts, when Molly Weasley battles Bellatrix Lestrange in DH. It's a feminine clash of the titans, pitting our favorite domestic goddess against Voldemort's scarlet woman. Molly the Earth Mother unleashes all the repressed hostility she has saved up over years while watching the Weasley clock turn to "mortal peril" for her loved ones, and her revenge is particularly sweet. She is standing up for Gideon and Fabian Prewett, whom Harry saw in a photograph of Order Members. We learn that Fabian and Gideon died heroically along with their parents in OotP, and J.K.R. wrote on her official site that they were Molly's twin brothers. She's also grieving the loss of her own twin son, Fred, and she doesn't want to lose anymore children to a senseless death. She's especially scared for her only daughter Ginny, who has been a target of the dark forces since CoS, when she is possessed by Tom Riddle's creepy diary-crux. Bellatrix has also gone after Ginny before, offering to torture the girl at the Department of Mysteries in OotP because Ginny is the smallest of the group. That happens just before Bella pushes Harry's godfather, Sirius, through the Death Veil. So for both Ginny and Harry, Molly is like an avenging angel, going after an evil witch who just won't stop.

As women, Molly and Bellatrix are opposites. Molly is the loyal wife to Arthur and a loving mother to her children. Bellatrix apparently dumps her husband Rodolphus Lestrange out of a sick obsession with Voldemort, and J.K.R. said at Carnegie Hall that Bellatrix is actually in love with the Dark Lord. Molly, on the other hand, would never be attracted to someone evil (although she has a soft spot for the wayward Gilderoy Lockhart in CoS), and she wants to adopt the entire world, taking care of Harry and Hermione both in OotP, and trying to help Tonks with her problems in HBP. Auntie Bella has no sympathy and would have gladly handed her nephew Draco over to the Dark Lord. She also doesn't seem to understand in HBP why Narcissa would be upset about losing her son that way, since it's an honor to please the Dark Lord [HBP, p. 35]. Bellatrix even says that if she had children of her own, she would have sacrificed them as well. Molly represents normal family life, while Bella is outside of society and nothing can control her.

Unlike Harry in the Priori Incantatum duel in GoF, Molly is an adult and knows exactly what she is doing. She's not afraid or at least doesn't show it if she is. She doesn't have a lucky wand or blood protection, and she's running only on adrenaline and motherly instinct, like every other mom in the series, from Lily to Narcissa. She gets the job done with one of the strongest and most colorful lines in the whole series: "Not my daughter, you bitch!" [p. 736]. That says it all, in spades. This is a big duel, and it overshadows the vanquishing of Voldemort at the end, which is all talk but little action. No other duel can compare with this one.

The Final Duel Between Voldemort and Harry (DH)

In GoF, Voldemort makes a long speech before dueling Harry, but this time in DH the tables are turned, and Harry returns the favor by explaining all the Dark Lord's mistakes over the years in minute detail, telling Voldemort "it's backfired on you, Riddle" [p. 742]. Like Dumbledore at the Ministry, Harry talks about the L-word, love, which is something Voldemort never wants to hear about, and points out that Snape was never on his side due to his love for Lily Potter, the very woman who had vanquished Voldemort when Harry was a baby. As Harry evokes the names of Lily, Snape, and Dumbledore, Voldemort gets more and more shaken up that their protection of Harry has foiled his evil plans again.

It's absolutely Harry's duel to lose because as Harry explains: While Voldemort is using the Elder Wand that he stole from Dumbledore's grave, the wand actually recognizes Harry as its true master because Harry overpowered Draco, the real master, weeks before. Plus, Harry has already (kind of) died and come back, so unlike Voldemort, he has no fear of death, and he has nearly become master of death by using the other two Hallows: the Cloak of Invisibility and the Resurrection Stone. The last Hallow he must use is the Elder Wand, but Harry doesn't even have to use the killing curse, *Avada Kedavra*. He uses good old *Expelliarmus*, the Disarming Charm, and things quickly happen, one, two, three: The Elder Wand lets Voldemort's own killing curse rebound on him so that it flies into Harry's hand because of *Expelliarmus*, and Voldemort falls down stone-cold dead. Everyone cheers and Harry's long ordeal is finally over. It is probably the shortest duel in the series, and it's not that exciting, but Harry is so in control of things that Voldemort has no chance at all, and that makes it a total victory.

Verdict

Harry duels Voldemort twice—trapped in the graveyard when he is fourteen in GoF, and again at Hogwarts when he is seventeen in DH. Both times it's a war of words ending with special-effect wands and a single Expelliarmus. *Dumbledore at the Ministry seemed like an easy mark, but he fights like a warrior and Voldemort has to flee. Talk about clash of the titans! And let's not forget when the women rocked it out—in the duel between Molly Weasley and Bellatrix Lestrange, two mature witches fight a classic skirmish between good and evil that is watched by hundreds of bystanders at that Battle of Hogwarts. Which duel is the best? Harry uses the Elder Wand's power in the final duel, as Dumbledore does at the Ministry. And in GoF, there is that whole* Priori Incantatum *thing in which the phoenix wands connect, giving Harry a chance to get out of there. However, a truly great duel should be more about talent and skill than tricky wands that kill with a single spell. Verdict: The duel between Dumbledore and Voldemort is the definition of epic.*

Who helps Harry more on his quest: Ron or Hermione?

Ron

In Book One, the first friend Harry makes on the train to Hogwarts is Ron Weasley, and they become best buds for life. They understand each other instantly, the way kids so often do. Harry sees a kindred soul in Ron, who also wears hand-me-down clothes and can't afford Chocolate Frogs [SS, p. 101]. Ron simply accepts Harry with his scar and all even when everyone else seems to avoid him like the plague. Oh sure, they argue now and then as best friends do, but that's because it is difficult for Ron to be in the shadow of the most famous wizard alive. It's a lot easier for Hermione to be the gal pal because she never has to compete with Harry, either at Quidditch or for popularity. And Ron is used to competing against his older brothers, so it's part of his personality, along with his temper. But whenever Harry really needs him, such as when the rest of the wizarding world turns on Harry in OotP, Ron is there to be supportive and watch his back. It's also because of Ron that Harry experiences magical family life, and the Weasleys nearly adopt Harry as one of their own. So Ron and Harry grow up almost as brothers.

It may sometimes seem that Hermione is the better friend because her rational plans so often get the Trio out of trouble, but sometimes Harry just wants someone to agree with him and not point out the flaws of all his ideas. Because Hermione's mind is so sharp, Ron doesn't always get credit when he *does* have a flash of brilliance, like when he wins the life-sized chess match in Book One. Except for his trouble with Apparating, Ron is just as magical as Hermione. At least he remembers that he is a wizard, while Hermione gets emotional in stressful times and falls into Muggle ways. She's unable to light a fire with her wand when the Trio is captured by the Devil's Snare plant on their way to finding the Sorcerer's Stone, for instance.

Ron gains depth as the series goes along, learning truths about love and loyalty and how to find his way back from despair after running away in anger. He is also heroic, saving Harry's life in DH by diving into freezing water, then destroying a Horcrux with the Sword of Gryffindor [DH, p. 377]. It may seem that Ron exists just to say silly things and not do his homework, but Harry needs these moments to lighten up and just be a kid. That's always the problem with Hermione—she's too serious and judgmental. Harry can't just sit around worrying all the time the way she does, and Ron is always there to have a sword fight with trick wands or to play a game of Exploding Snap. That's what best friends are for.

Hermione

Basically, Ron is a goof who is good with one-liners, but he is often missing in action during important times in Harry's life. Hermione is the one who is Harry's true friend and advisor. She helps him more than anyone else in the series. For one thing, without Hermione to help him study, Harry would never pass his classes, and that goes for Ron as well. Ron is useless at helping Harry figure out the mystery of Nicholas Flamel and the Sorcerer's Stone in Book One, which Hermione figures out on her own at the library. She also solves the puzzle of the basilisk in CoS just before she is Petrified [CoS, p. 290]. Ron, on the other hand, can't even fathom that his rat is really the evil Peter Pettigrew in dumpy Animagus form, and he certainly never guesses that Lupin is a werewolf the way Hermione does, which goes to show that she is the "cleverest witch of [her] age" [PoA, p. 346].

Speaking of clever ideas, who has the idea that Harry should teach Defense Against the Dark Arts (DADA) to Dumbledore's Army? Hermione, of course. Who knows that the Half-Blood Prince's book might be darker than it seems while the boys just laugh it up about Harry accidentally using the *Levicorpus* spell to hang Ron up in the air in HBP? Hermione. And who rescues Harry and Ron with Apparition in *Deathly Hallows*? Hermione again. Ron just can't multitask the way Hermione does, and he is so emotionally immature that he lets Harry down by constantly being jealous and overly sensitive.

Ron is petty during the Triwizard Tournament in GoF. He runs away in anger from their task in Deathly Hallows (and can't find his way back). Hermione, who loves Ron, could have run after him, but she stays with Harry because he needs her as a friend, and they have important work to do. Hermione is with Harry at Christmas in Godric's Hollow, which is one of the most emotional scenes ever, when Harry comes to terms with the deaths of his parents. Hermione is there to explain the theory of life after death, almost like a spiritual advisor. Ron, who isn't there, can't be much help, and that's symbolic of the whole problem. Most of the time, Hermione and Harry have to keep on going in spite of Ron's temper tantrums and whiny behavior. They can get by just fine without him. In contrast to Ron, Hermione never falls apart or forgets how much Harry needs her. She doesn't let petty differences among the Trio get in the way of their mission to defeat Voldemort.

It's really unfair that while Hermione saves Harry from the giant snake and the Dark Lord in DH, Ron suddenly pops back into the story to wield the Sword of Gryffindor and get the glory of smashing the locket Horcrux [DH, p. 377]. He doesn't deserve that glory since he basically betrayed both his friends by leaving in the first place. Hermione never thought of leaving even once, yet she forgives Ron for abandoning them, so she represents the true meaning of friendship.

Verdict

Ron is the classic friend of the hero, loyal and funny, if not always the brightest light. Hermione is the brain of the Trio, but her generous heart teaches Harry about forgiveness and human nature. Verdict: Ron is a brave companion, but Hermione never turns her back on Harry. Harry couldn't have defeated Voldemort without help from both of them, but the verdict is: We ship Harry/Hermione. (In a matter of speaking.)

Are the movie studios splitting Deathly Hallows *into two parts for strictly financial reasons?*

No!

The studios wouldn't split up an important movie just for the money—they really do care about the fans so they are trying to make sure that everyone's favorite scenes won't end up on the cutting room floor. It's impossible to pack everything from such a long book into one movie, and it would so sad if anything were left out. DH is a critically important book because it ties everything together. All the subplots and backstories have to be included or the series as a whole won't make any sense. And remember—not everyone who goes to the theater has read all the books. People will be totally confused if elements such as the Elder Wand and the Horcruxes are not explained at length. Also, important details about Lily, Snape, Dumbledore, Grindelwald, and the events of Godric's Hollow might be lost. So creatively, the only answer is to double our fun and give us everything in two movies.

The studios also know that two shorter movies stand a better chance of being carried by the majority of theaters. When a cineplex carries a four-hour epic, it is usually shown only on limited screens or at night. It just doesn't make sense to make the fans drive around looking for the one place within fifty miles that chooses to carry an ultra-long movie. Even superfans don't have time off from work or school to sit and watch a *Titanic*–length DH over and over.

And viewers want all the special effects, but in a shortened DH, something would have to go. Otherwise, the movie would be too expensive to make. Should they skimp on the seven flying Potters battle scene or the Battle of Hogwarts? Should they leave out the dragon or the giants? Who can decide? Some things have to stay in: Ralph Fiennes's nose has to be blurred out in every scene, fight scenes have to be blazing with fiery spells, the giant snake has to float around in a bubble and bite Snape in the throat, and that's a lot of levitation and fake blood. All of these effects will be so much better if the studios don't have to hurry through and skimp on the money, and the fans win.

The studios want to create something for the ages that people will watch twenty years from now. Fans waited years between books, so they'll be glad to wait six months between movies. The payoff will be a twin set of movies that are true to the books, with all the little details we love so much. This is the last time we will sit in the dark and wait for the movie magic, and the studios want to be sure they get it right.

Yes!

Let's not kid ourselves—this is all about the money. Warner Bros. is a business, and the purpose of a business is to make money. Why make people pay once when they can make them pay twice? They'll get double the box-office receipts and double the payments for DVDs, calendars, and poster books. Warner Bros. knows fans will see both movies, regardless of how outraged some claim to be.

DH is actually shorter than some of the other books—OotP is longer but was gutted for the big screen. This is the last book and the last chance the studios have to make mega-Muggle-bucks, and they know the fans will pay up in order to see the grand finale.

Of course, the studios say they are really doing this for "artistic reasons." But if that's true, why didn't they know which scene would be the cutoff point for the first movie? If they had it planned out "artistically," they would already know whether to split it after Godric's Hollow or after Malfoy Manor. The fact that the producer and the writer couldn't decide right away means that the decision was based on accounting spreadsheets and not creativity.

The studios say that theater owners won't go along with a four-hour movie anymore, but that's absurd—look at recent movies, such as the *Lord of the Rings* trilogy, which were blockbusters making millions of dollars worldwide. Warner Bros. knows that some fans—like the kind reading this book—won't mind spending a whole day (or night) at the movie theater seeing DH once (or even twice—or more). But they know that there are millions of casual fans who *would* mind—think parents and families. Small children? Forget it.

In every other movie so far, the studios have cut out huge chunks of the story from the books and added filler they think is better. In PoA the Shrunken Heads take up more time than the Marauder's backstory. In GoF, the dragon was more important than the return of Sirius Black, and in OotP, we had a lot of Umbridge and Filch, but very little of "Snape's Worst Memory" (not even on the DVD). Already, characters such as Fleur Delacour and Madame Trelawney have been left out of HBP, and they've added an extra scene about an attack on the Burrow, which wasn't in the book. If they will change so much in a two-hour movie, shouldn't we expect the same in each half of DH? The answer is yes. WB's job as a business is to entertain the casual fans, vast in numbers, and placate the serious fans—or at least not alienate them. They will do whatever they think is best to the plot, charge us twice, and know that the serious fans will see the movies anyway. It's not about movie magic, but money magic—and this strategy is how WB brings home the Benjamins to shareholders.

Verdict

It will be quite an achievement for Warner Bros. to swish out a flick that captures the complicated essence of DH. The fans want it all and the attention to detail has to be impeccable. Of course, the studios can't commit a Sectumsempra *of the plot points or the fans will raise a ruckus forever. However, Warner Bros. is a business—its sole reason for existence in a capitalist system is to maximize profits. Both views are correct: WB is splitting DH both to make more money and to ensure justice is done to the final book in the series. It's a win-win.*

What is the most shocking moment in the series?

Voldemort's Return (GoF)

When Voldemort tried to kill Harry as a baby, the killing curse rebounded, destroying the Dark Lord's body and reducing his soul to the size of a microbe. Everyone knew he would return someday, bigger and badder than ever, but nobody was quite prepared for the way in which it happened.

Voldie's first attempts at reanimation, by possessing Professor Quirrell and Ginny Weasley, both fail. The third time is the charm, so to speak, and the one that disgusted and shocked readers everywhere. Voldemort's most faithful servant, Wormtail (aka Peter Pettigrew), finds the Dark Lord in Albania and is able to get him halfway to bodily form by animating a deformed baby (the magic used to create this baby is never described in the books, but the author said in an interview that she grossed out her editor by explaining it once [JKR-PC1]).

Peter nurses the horrible creature with snake venom to nourish Voldemort's soul inside so that it will be prepared to find its true form in the climactic graveyard scene of GoF. Readers were caught off guard by this scene because one moment they're reading breathlessly as Harry navigates the maze of the Triwizard Cup, and the next—after Harry and Cedric Diggory touch the Portkey—they're in the graveyard surrounded by Voldemort's Death Eaters. Suddenly, Cedric Diggory is dead and Harry is bound and gagged at the mercy of Voldemort. But nothing could prepare readers for what came next. Wormtail shockingly tosses the deformed baby into a boiling cauldron. He then throws in a bone from Voldemort's dead father along with some of Harry's blood before sickeningly cutting off his own right hand and throwing it into the disgusting boiling brew. From that noxious cauldron of dark magic, the Dark Lord rises again, just as evil and snakelike as ever, giving readers their first terrifying glimpse of Voldemort back from the dead and ready to begin a new reign of terror.

The Death of Sirius Black (OotP)

The biggest shocker of all time is the deadly moment when Sirius Black suddenly falls through the Death Veil at the Department of Mysteries. Few expected Sirius to die, and nobody expected his death to be so sudden and anticlimactic! Who would ever think that such a major character so attached to Harry would just suddenly disappear off the face of the earth without warning? Sirius had everything to live for. He was handsome, funny, and intelligent. Being Harry's godfather gave him a family and brought him joy. He had wasted so many years in Azkaban for a crime he never committed, and after that he was trapped as a fugitive in Grimmauld Place. Everyone hoped the Ministry would clear his good name so he could have a real life and watch Harry grow up. The fight at the Ministry was his first real chance in years to get into some dueling action for the Order of the Phoenix, zapping the Death Eaters right and left. Then BAM! Cousin Bellatrix gets in one lucky shot and Sirius, Harry's mentor and father figure, falls backward into the Veil of Death [OotP, p. 806].

People still can't believe it happened—it was the worst surprise in all the books. By the time Lupin kept Harry from jumping through the veil after Sirius, people realized he was really dead. Many fans were sobbing at that point. Others threw their books at the wall. How could it happen? Maybe it was just a trick and Sirius would return in the next book. Maybe Harry would figure out how to use the magic mirror that Sirius and James used to use during detentions to bring Sirius back. Maybe Harry would return to the veil and find a way to revive him. He couldn't really be dead, could he? But no—it was over for the ex-Marauder. The Order lost a warrior hero, the wizarding world lost the last of the Blacks, fans lost their favorite shaggy Animagus, and Harry lost the father figure who loved him most. Why was it necessary? Why couldn't Sirius go out fighting with Lupin in Book Seven? Sirius died too young, too soon, all too shockingly.

The Death of Dumbledore (HBP)

As startling as Sirius's death was, nothing compares to the shock of the way in which Dumbledore was killed in HBP. Fans were warned beforehand that something major was coming, and we thought we were prepared. Boy, were we wrong! First of all, hardly anyone thought Dumbledore would get the ax—he was too important to the story, too close to Harry—he was the headmaster of Hogwarts and the best wizard in the world, for crying out loud. But even those prescient few who saw it coming could never have predicted *how* Dumbledore died.

In HBP, fans were finally starting to get used to the idea that Snape, as much of a jerk as he was, was actually a good guy trying to protect Harry. But then, in that final, fateful scene at Hogwarts, as Dumbledore stands there weaponless and surrounded by Death Eaters, he looks to Snape and cries "Severus, please." Readers assumed that Snape would rise to the occasion and blast the Death Eaters away. We were oh so wrong! Snape took one look at Dumbledore and blasted him right off the Astronomy Tower. How could he!? He was supposed to be a good guy! And now Dumbledore, Harry's strongest ally, was dead and gone... forever. Fans were stunned with grief and couldn't put the puzzle together in their minds.

Verdict

Voldemort's life never ceases to amaze (or repulse) us, and fans reacted strongly when he appeared as a reptilian baby in GoF, and then—even more so—when they first saw him emerge as his fully formed, snakelike self. Sirius and Dumbledore both fall to their deaths suddenly—one disappears through the mysterious veil, another tumbles off a high tower. The hearts of the fans fell with them, and the shockwaves still reverberate from unexpectedly losing two beloved characters. But which moment left readers stunned the most? Verdict: It's a tough call, but nothing had fans flipping back pages to reread faster than Sirius's sudden death. At least Dumbledore went out with some fanfare.

Which character is most surprising?

Mad-Eye Moody/Barty Crouch, Jr.

Harry has quite a memorable and surprising fourth year at Hogwarts in GoF with the Triwizard Tournament going on, but he has a great Defense Against the Dark Arts teacher to help him prepare for the contest—Professor Mad-Eye Moody. Or, at least he thinks it's Mad-Eye Moody. In fact, the crusty, old Auror is Death Eater Barty Crouch, Jr., hopped up on Polyjuice Potion. So when Professor Moody is supposed to be teaching the kids about the Unforgiveable Curses, he is actually enjoying their horrified responses. When he puts Harry and others under the Imperius Curse, it is because Death Eaters like to control people. When he is nice to Neville, Crouch/Mad-Eye is really remembering that he helped the Lestranges drive the boy's parents insane with the Cruciatus Curse. Fake Moody does it all to help deliver Harry to the Dark Lord.

At the beginning of the Third Task of the Tournament, Moody leads Harry into the symbolic and dangerous maze that could have spelled death for the young wizard, but Harry outduels the Dark Lord and returns to Hogwarts. And guess who is there waiting for him? Professor Moody, who gets Harry away from everyone and then starts to freak out from lack of the Polyjuice, unable to avoid the Death Eater urge to brag about his evil plan. Surprise! The real Moody is locked in a dungeon down inside Barty Jr.'s magical trunk and has to be saved by Dumbledore. It's such an impressive masquerade that most readers forget that, that year, Professor Moody was not the real Moody at all.

Severus Snape

Professor Snape's character is always so sarcastic and nasty to Harry, Hermione, and Neville that quite a few Harry Potter readers started looking forward to Snape's long, slow, painful death, even wondering how quickly

Harry would kill him off in DH out of revenge for the death of Dumbledore. But, surprisingly, it doesn't turn out that way at all. In fact, Snape never was as heartless as he seemed, nor was he out to be top Death Eater in Lord Voldemort's service, the way Bellatrix and Draco thought in HBP. He's Dumbledore's man through and through and never intends to kill the headmaster. He even worries that it will destroy his own soul if he commits murder. Wow—Severus Snape with a spiritual side? Imagine him in a church pew wearing his Sunday best.

And the reason he turns against the Dark Side in the first place is one of the biggest surprises of the series: He loves the girl next door, Lily Evans, who grew up to be Harry's mother. Snape's request to spare her life is the only reason Lily is given a choice to either step away from Harry or die. And, of course, Lily did choose to die, which is the reason for other surprising scenes of Snape weeping over her death and weeping over an old letter. When Harry sees Snape's memories, he finally understands, and he takes the surprising role as Snape's champion in front of the whole school, the Death Eaters, and Lord Voldemort. It's an astonishing plot twist for the ages.

Draco Malfoy

Draco is always just the stereotyped school bully at Hogwarts and the pureblood Slytherin opposite of Harry, so it was a big surprise that we actually began to care about his fate in HBP. The catalyst for change in his character first comes about at the end of OotP, when Dumbledore tosses Draco's wealthy and powerful father into Azkaban. After that, Draco is mad at the world and determined to join forces with Voldemort to get back at Harry and the Order of the Phoenix. But it all backfires, leaving Draco alone with his problems in HBP, pouring out his sadness to none other than the ghostly Moaning Myrtle. Being a Death Eater is more like torture than some glorious quest, plus Voldemort's price for not following orders is certain death. And the assignment from the Dark Lord is not exactly for a beginner: Draco has to figure out a way to kill Headmaster Dumbledore. Trying to become a murderer nearly drives Draco to despair, especially when his plans keep failing and others such as Katie Bell and Ron Weasley are hurt during the attempts.

The surprise is not that Draco's life goes down the wrong path, but that he regrets it so quickly. He is smart enough to realize something his parents never taught him—that serving the Dark Lord is a dead-end job, just as Regulus Black and Severus Snape learned years before. Draco never wants to kill Dumbledore, and when push comes to shove, he can't do it. He doesn't seem too thrilled either when Voldemort kills Charity Burbage, the Muggle Studies teacher, before his eyes in DH; in fact, he can't bear to look at her. And more importantly, even though Draco recognizes the Trio at Malfoy Manor, he doesn't blow their cover to the Death Eaters or even his own parents, which is what he would have done before his own suffering began. That's especially amazing since Harry almost kills Draco with the *Sectumsempra* spell the year before in HBP, and they hate each other's guts. So Draco is just not the evil kid that he seems, and it is justice that he survives the Battle of Hogwarts.

Plus, Tom Felton is so dreamy.

Narcissa Malfoy

Narcissa Malfoy is the big surprise of the series because who would expect to sympathize with a rich, pureblood snob who has her nose in the air? Her son is a spoiled-brat bully, her husband is a Death Eater, and her abused house-elf Dobby ran away from home. Yet, over the course of the last two books in the series, we learn that she, surprisingly, has a heart and it is breaking because she has nearly lost Draco to the Dark Lord. She may be Bellatrix Lestrange's sister, but she's as different from her sister as night and day. Narcissa stays loyal to her husband even when he is in Azkaban, and she is willing to risk the anger of Voldemort to save her only son. In HBP, she sees the good in her friend Severus Snape, trusting him as the only one of the Death Eaters who will help her in her time of grief. Who would have guessed that Narcissa would show a vulnerable, emotional side?

Of course, she's not perfect. She has no love for any children but her own and gives Harry a tongue-lashing about his chances of survival. She also tricks Snape into making an Unbreakable Vow to finish off Dumbledore, which is not nice considering he was so chivalrous to her. But, in the end, she wants to save Draco's life so much in DH that she lies to the Dark Lord, telling him that Harry is dead when she knows he is alive. Her only goal is to get back to Hogwarts and see Draco again. Narcissa shows unexpected strength and courage under torture from Voldemort, and she has the right family values to bring down the Dark Lord. Like her cousins Regulus and Sirius, and her sister Andromeda, Narcissa symbolizes all the good things about the Noble and Most Ancient house of Black. She turns out to be semi-likable—who would have expected that?

Dudley Dursley

No one expected any changes in Harry's cousin Dudley Dursley, since he's been beating up on Harry all his life while growing up on Privet Drive. He is the classic big bully and kids like him don't change, right? Well, think again. Whether Dudley changes because the Dementor nearly sucks out his soul in OotP, or just because he is growing up, we find out in DH that he actually cares about Harry. How can this be true?

Hasn't the Big D always put himself first? He is the essence of selfish stupidity and gluttony and the biggest juvenile delinquent on the playground. Wouldn't he be glad to know that his rival cousin Harry is out of his life forever? Apparently not. When Aunt Petunia is ready to walk away from Harry in DH without a backward glance, Dudley actually shows some decency and waits to say goodbye to his cousin, plus he thanks him for saving his life a few years before in OotP. It is one of the most touching scenes in the books, and it's a complete surprise. Harry can't believe what he is hearing—Dudley has a heart after all. It's a jaw-dropping moment—who would have thought it was possible?

Verdict

Mad-Eye Moody surprises even his old friend Dumbledore when he turns out to be Barty Jr. in disguise. Severus Snape, Draco Malfoy, and his mother Narcissa are those rare Slytherins who chose love over power. Dudley Dursley is the idiotic bully who suddenly seems sorry for his cousin Harry in a rare display of emotion. Who surprised readers the most? Most believe there is some good in everybody, so Draco, Narcissa, and Dudley are out of the running. Many people—us included— predicted Snape's true mission. So Snape is out, too. While each of these characters teach Harry not to judge someone by outward appearances, Barty Crouch Jr. surprises even Dumbledore. Verdict: Nobody could have predicted Barty Crouch Jr.'s identity; he is the most surprising character in the books.

Should the love potion Amortentia be illegal?

Yes!

The powerful elixir of love known as Amortentia should be banned from the wizarding world for a very good reason—the only thing it does is make someone fall in love against their will. That's why the Merope Riddle story in HBP is so pathetically sick: She used Amortentia to trick her Muggle boyfriend, Tom, into marrying her, and then kept him drugged up for the entire time they were together. Dumbledore refers to the relationship as a form of enslavement. No one knows exactly where Merope got the idea. It's possible that Amortentia had been used for arranged pureblood marriages through the centuries. Otherwise, how would nasty people such as her father, Marvolo Gaunt, ever find a wife? But that doesn't make it right, and it should not be legal.

Merope's love is one-sided, and Tom Riddle Sr. has no choice in the matter—the potion completely takes over his mind. That's not very different from the Imperius Curse, which Harry learns in GoF is an illegal spell that gives a wizard total control over another person. Similarly, Amortentia takes away a person's free will and ability to make decisions. It's true that Merope tries to give Tom his freedom when she finds out they are expecting a baby, but by then it is too late and he has been tricked for too long. No wonder he runs from her and never wants to see his son. Who could learn to love someone dishonest enough to use a love potion? And their son turns out to be the most evil wizard of all time, so Amortentia caused major problems for the next generation.

It's also doubly wrong for a love potion to be available at a school such as Hogwarts, with all the teenage hormones floating around. The temptation for abuse is too great. Look what happens in HBP when Romilda Vane aims for Harry with her spiked Chocolate Cauldrons, but doses Ron accidentally. He becomes head over heels in love while under the influence of a girl he doesn't even like [HBP, p. 392]. Fred and George Weasley may have done good business selling obsessive love in a bottle, but it is never going to replace the real thing. True, it has a pleasant smell, but infatuation is too addictive. J.K.R. said during an interview that there is a Love Room at the Department of Mysteries filled with a vat of the potion, but it is kept behind a locked door for safety. That's fine if wizards are using it for controlled research about love, but in the wrong hands, Amortentia confuses people and can lead to broken hearts and tragic Vegas-shotgun weddings.

No!

There's no need to ban Amortentia. Only Dark Magic is illegal in the wizarding world, and Amortentia is *not* Dark. If it was so bad, why would the Ministry keep a vat of it around, and why would Horace Slughorn be allowed to teach the potion in his class? Why would it have the pleasant scent that is different for each person, such as the honeysuckle that reminds Harry of Ginny? Most of the time, Amortentia is just a harmless potion that wears off in less than a day. It's all part of adolescent mischief in the wizarding world. Molly Weasley laughingly tells Ginny and Hermione in PoA about the time she made a love potion while growing up, and yet she finds true love with Arthur later on. Her experience doesn't influence Ginny and Hermione to trick Ron and Harry that way. Ron is not mortally damaged by the bad experience with Romilda Vane, either. He actually hurts Hermione's feelings more with Lavender Brown, who didn't use a love potion to get his attention [HBP, p. 302].

Merope Riddle is an extreme case, and there are obvious reasons why she abuses Amortentia. It's similar to a troubled teenager using drugs in the Muggle world. Merope is never loved by her horrible family who keep her isolated out in the woods. She has no friends and no Hogwarts education—her father calls her a Squib and shouts at her. Then there is her appearance, which would turn off any possible boyfriends—eyes turned in opposite directions and a ragged appearance, not to mention a Parseltongue voice that hisses like a snake. Wouldn't any girl want love from the only decent boy she knew, even if he was a Muggle and she was a witch? That doesn't make it right that she uses a love potion, but who is to say she didn't deserve what little happiness she had on earth through using Amortentia?

Most potions are legal in the wizarding world, even if they are restricted in certain situations. If they ban Amortentia, they might as well ban

Polyjuice or Felix Felicis, too. Each witch or wizard has to grow up and learn to use them responsibly, and the Ministry should stay out of it.

Verdict

As singer Celestina Warbeck croons over the wizarding wireless in HBP, there's nothing like a "cauldron full of hot strong love." Should Amortentia stay legal so that unattractive witches like Merope Riddle can catch a husband? Or should it be banned to protect teenagers from becoming more lovesick and confused than usual? Verdict: Love is always the answer in the Potterverse, but the potion Amortentia is much too potent and should be illegal.

What is the most useful potion?

Felix Felicis

If someone has luck on their side, they've got it all, so the most useful potion is Felix Felicis, the golden liquid that Harry wins as a prize in HBP. Nothing else helps Harry as much, especially in learning to trust his own instincts and powers of persuasion. When Harry uses Felix Felicis and follows the small voice within, things always turn out for the best. With it, he is able to get the memory of young Tom Riddle from Slughorn, which proves that there are multiple Horcruxes. Without Felix Felicis, Harry might not have known how to defeat Voldemort, so it's really the most important potion in the series.

Felix Felicis is something like self-confidence in a bottle or a psychological booster shot. Even the very thought of it is powerful, as Harry proves when he pretends to put a drop in Ron's pumpkin juice in HBP, turning his best friend into Mr. Super Quidditch so he can play a perfect game. Professor Slughorn also tells the class that taking Felix gave him two perfect days in his life. It's possible that having the potion around helps Harry realize he is in love with Ginny in HBP. Who knows? Without Felix Felicis, Harry and Ginny might not have had such a happy ending.

Harry is able to generously share the Felix potion with other members of Dumbledore's Army in HBP and that saves their lives in the fight with the Death Eaters. People who might have otherwise died are able to survive and help Harry in the future. That includes Snape and Draco, who never take the potion but whose escapes from the Order are lucky for everyone involved because they turn out to be less evil than Harry previously believed. Any potion that can save that many lives is the most useful potion of all.

Polyjuice Potion

One of the most useful weapons the Order of the Phoenix has against the Death Eaters in DH is made in a cauldron: Polyjuice Potion, which is used to make a person look like someone else, so it's useful for disguise. Felix Felicis may be sparkly and lucky, but it's also rare and takes months to make. Too much of it can make someone reckless and ill, as Slughorn warns the kids in HBP. But even a child can make and use Polyjuice Potion, as Hermione proves in CoS, when she cooks up a batch in Moaning Myrtle's bathroom. The uses are endless, from childhood pranks to spying during wartime, and come in handy for the Trio in DH several times. All you need is a hair from someone's head, and you can distill the essence of a person and assume another identity [CoS, p. 159]. Of course, some versions, like those made by Crabbe or Bellatrix, taste icky or oniony. And you don't want any cat hairs in your Polyjuice or you might end up with a tail and whiskers, as Hermione accidentally does in CoS. But Polyjuice is extremely versatile, helping people to disguise themselves by changing their gender, size, and age. Since most wizards don't have Metamorphmagus abilities like Nymphadora Tonks, Polyjuice is the next best thing.

Sure, we see abuses of the potion, as when Barty Crouch, Jr. steals the identity of Mad-Eye Moody in GoF, or when Crabbe changes into a little girl so he can spy for Draco in HBP. Polyjuice is also somewhat limited because the effects only last about an hour, and you have to keep drinking it continuously for the disguise to last. But the usefulness overcomes any drawbacks. Harry and the Trio successfully take on other identities to get into the Ministry in DH to take back Slytherin's locket from Umbridge, and with Hermione disguised as Bellatrix Lestrange, they manage to get into the vault at Gringotts to find Helga Hufflepuff's cup. In the last case, they also rescue a tortured dragon that has been chained by the goblins and fly him out the front door.

The best use of the Polyjuice Potion in DH is the scheme of the seven Potters, when seven of Harry's friends take Polyjuice Potion to look just like him in order to be decoys as they fly Harry to safety. It's interesting that Harry's own personal form of Polyjuice is a bright golden color, which is the same color as Felix Felicis. Perhaps the message is that Harry was born with a lucky essence anyway, so Felix Felicis doesn't really matter. In DH, all the seven Potters survive, even if their escorts do not, and they are protected by Essence of Harry. Masking their true identities is what saves their lives, and that's all due to Polyjuice Potion, the most useful of all.

Verdict

Both potions are helpful to Harry. The bottle of Felix Felicis gives him a gold standard for success and teaches Harry to trust the voice within. Polyjuice Potion gives Harry and friends the power of disguise, which is the key to many successful missions. Verdict: Harry is lucky even without Felix Felicis, but the Order Members couldn't have changed their appearances and slip past Death Eaters without Polyjuice Potion, making it the most useful.

Which is the best book?

It's a tricky subject to choose a best book, since each one is a stepping stone to the next in the series. And every fan has a different opinion, so bear with us—this next section is completely subjective!

Goblet of Fire

There's a sporty and light-hearted feeling to much of GoF, and one thing that puts this book above the rest is that Harry discovers there is magic all over the world, which broadens his horizons. At the Quidditch World Cup he sees wizards from Africa, Ireland, and the United States. Later in the Triwizard Tournament at Hogwarts, there are students from Durmstrang and Beauxbatons, representing the countries of Bulgaria and France. Harry even learns about other creatures not seen in other books, from the Merpeople to the Sphinx in the tournament maze. Also, this book introduces a new human character on almost every page, from the amazing Quidditch hero Viktor Krum to the gruff and suspicious Mad-Eye Moody, to the outrageous news reporter Rita Skeeter and her poisonous green quill. Other favorite characters return, such as Sirius Black, who is hiding out in a cave as the dog Snuffles, and Dobby the house-elf, who is free and working at Hogwarts. Dumbledore is there, of course, as Harry's wise and kindly mentor, and happily in GoF, their relationship is not as dark and emotionally heated as it becomes in later books.

Harry finds himself in a unique situation in GoF because even though he is the hero of the books, he is not the only champion at Hogwarts, and that's refreshing. Fame is not what it's cracked up to be. For once, he realizes how much he still has to learn about magic, which is a better message than many of the books, which assume that Harry was born knowing exactly what to do in every situation. Viktor, Fleur Delacoeur, and Cedric Diggory are older and more sophisticated than Harry is, and Harry is thrown for a loop when he has to compete with them. His challenge is to discover his own strengths and talents with the help of his friends and then rise to the occasion.

Another superior quality of GoF is that Harry and his friends have some very typical teenage scenes that are funny and universal. There's a dance called the Yule Ball, and Harry works up the courage to invite his crush of the moment, Cho Chang, only to be bitterly disappointed that she is going with his rival Cedric. Ron overlooks inviting Hermione until it's too late, and then is jealous when he discovers that Viktor is her date and that he's been following her around the library. When the dance actually begins, Harry and Ron are completely clueless and thoughtless and don't want to dance with their actual partners, the Patil sisters. In spite of some rocking out by the band The Weird Sisters, the dance is a big letdown for the kids, but that's what makes it so recognizable and true to life.

But don't think that GoF is all fun and games—oh no. It's a mystery beginning with the gloomy and decrepit Riddle house, ancestral home of the Dark Lord. We learn about Tom Riddle's past and what happened to his doomed Muggle family. We learn lots of new details about Peter Pettigrew and Severus Snape, who are both Death Eaters but perhaps not always on the same side. GoF has one of the best grand finales of the series: a truly scary horror scene with the evil Voldemort in a graveyard making a wicked comeback from a big cauldron. After fighting one of the most exciting duels in the series, Harry barely escapes death only to come face to face with the best unexpected plot twist in the series—Mad-Eye Moody is not who he really seems to be! A great ending to a book that has it all.

Deathly Hallows

J. K. Rowling saved her best for last. Fans waited for so many years to read DH, and it turned out to be everything they hoped for. It answers all the mysteries. Who will die in the war with Voldemort? Is Severus Snape good or bad? Can the Order of the Phoenix go on without Dumbledore? Readers had been sitting in the dark, waiting in anticipation, and then DH came through and blew away all their expectations.

Harry is both at his most adult and most vulnerable in this book, more alone than ever and unsure of his own ability to vanquish the Dark Lord. It's so satisfying to see him grow older and more mature with each book, and the themes he is grappling with become more and more complex, never more so than in DH when Harry must finally face the biggest theme of them all: death. Death is ever present in this book and, in fact, Harry himself briefly "dies" when his soul floats off to King's Cross during his battle with Voldemort.

But the book isn't all heavy-handed seriousness. A ton of awesome new material is revealed, coming out of nowhere. Harry's quest is to search out and destroy the evil Horcruxes, but what about the mysterious Deathly Hallows and Dumbledore's own troubled past? What did the racist Grindelwald have to do with anything? Voldemort reaches his goal of a pureblood dictatorship, while kicking around his own followers. Will they mutiny or follow him to the bitter end? Surprising allies help Harry at crucial moments and teach him that, in the end, everyone can love and be human, despite the house affiliations and resentments. The battle scenes are spectacular, with giants and enormous spiders, centaurs and hippogriffs, flashy duels and agonizing deaths. But *Deathly Hallows* is the best book in the series at defining heroism and bravery, not just in terms of reckless deeds, but by redemptive acts and the power of remorse. Reading this book is like escaping on a flying dragon and landing in a sunlit meadow, knowing everything has turned out just as it should.

Prisoner of Azkaban

Forget *Deathly Hallows*—the best book in the series is *Prisoner of Azkaban*. Why? Because there is not a wasted word or unnecessary scene. It is a tightly wound mystery that has a beginning, middle, and end, and unlike some of the longer books, it is enjoyable as a novel all by itself. The plotline elegantly solves several problems at once and introduces two of the most important characters in Harry's life: Remus Lupin and Sirius Black. Clues are cleverly scattered around the hallways of Hogwarts and the streets of Hogsmeade. What is Lupin's mysterious ailment? Does Sirius Black really want to kill Harry? How is Hermione taking double classes? And why is Scabbers losing all his fur?

PoA has the best magical object of all time—the Marauder's Map— which is not only extremely useful, but amusing (after all, it entertained Fred and George for years, and they were always up to no good). Harry probably learns more in PoA than any other book, both in and out of class—how to destroy a Boggart, how to cope with Dementors, the difference between a Patronus and an Animagus, and several dark secrets from the past. We get backstory in spades, all about Harry's father, James, and his gang of mischievous teenage Marauders running through the moonlit forest of the past. Many old friends and foes meet again in the dramatic Shrieking Shack showdown. Throw in a hippogriff execution, shocking plot twists, a werewolf, and one of the best time-travel stories of all time, and no one could ask for more.

Verdict

Goblet of Fire *is a great rambling tale that has loads of action, from flying brooms to dangerous dragon-fighting, and the ending turns the key to solve several mysteries.* Deathly Hallows *is the book of revelations for the entire series, answering all questions and ending with an epic battle on the parapets of Hogwarts.* Prisoner of Azkaban *is an old-fashioned whodunit that twists and turns like the tunnel under the Whomping Willow. PoA is the most popular book in the series, according to the polls. But* Goblet of Fire *was our favorite.*

Is Voldemort the most evil fictional character ever?

No!

Voldemort just doesn't fit the bill as the "most evil" when compared to other fictional villains. For one thing, other characters in the Harry Potter series overshadow him—Dolores Umbridge or Fenrir Greyback, for instance, who are much more nightmarish, not to mention the Dementors. Voldemort also loves the sound of his own voice so much that the readers fall asleep waiting for the action. In every duel, he just stands there talking about what he is going to do. It's like Dr. Evil planning a drawn-out torture scene, when he could just shoot Austin Powers and have it over with. And the few times Voldemort gets angry, he's something like Al Capone in *The Untouchables*, ranting and raving until he seems ridiculous, and then hitting someone with a baseball bat (in Voldie's case, feeding a Muggle-born to his snake). It's a joke and more like a caricature of a bad guy.

In appearance, the Dark Lord most resembles a B-grade horror movie monster, such as *The Creature from the Black Lagoon*. He's part reptile after all. He's a bit like Jim Carrey in *The Mask*, who is more comical than frightening. He can't compare to the vampires of old, such as the elegant Dracula, who saves the bloodletting for an after-dinner drink, and who at least wear basic black. With his greenish tinge and lack of a nose, Voldemort resembles the demons from *Buffy the Vampire Slayer*, but no kickboxing is required to kill him. Harry doesn't even need a silver sword or wooden stake—he vanquishes Voldemort with pure sweet love and *Expelliarmus*. Unfortunately, the death scenes are really lame because the Dark Lord just falls over. It's a pity that he doesn't melt into a puddle of green goop like the Wicked Witch of the West in *The Wizard of Oz*, with a flying monkey there to check his pulse. That would be cool.

It's just wrong to compare Voldemort to truly scary villains like Darth Vader or Emperor Palpatine of *Star Wars*, who were once decent people but let evil corrupt them. Voldemort has no good in him and can't love anyone. His ancestors are inbred and his family abandons him, so he is wired from birth to be bad. At the orphanage, he hangs a bunny from the rafters, then he goes to Hogwarts where he reaches his full potential as a warped teenager. Even the Terminator and Frankenstein's monster could learn to love, but Voldemort never can. As a villain, he has no depth and is just a cardboard bad guy. He stands up; Harry knocks him down. The end.

Yes!

Voldemort is the most evil villain ever, period. Look at his main goal—he likes to hunt down and kill babies. He tortures people for fun until they scream. He's like the devil in every horror story, putting the Dark Mark on his followers who bow to him. He's the nightmare kid who hates his mother and kills his father.

When he is a boy, Tom is only suspected by Dumbledore, who thinks Tom might have a bad side. The teenager completely fools his head of house, Horace Slughorn, in a performance worthy of psycho Norman Bates. Later, when he is vanquished and out of sight, Voldemort is still so frightening that people dare not speak his name, much like the fear caused by the Eye of Sauron from *Lord of the Rings*. But Sauron never appears in human form and stays far away in Mordor. By contrast, Voldemort is restless and on the prowl, possessing Ginny Weasley and Professor Quirrell—transforming from a mere speck to a hideous venom-drinking baby. His final form of a man with a greenish face like a snake and red catlike eyes is weirder than any other villain in literature.

Voldemort is much worse than the bad guys in *Star Wars*. It's true that he uses people in government to gain power like Emperor Palpatine, but the Dark Lord makes sure his apprentices won't turn on him. He is always the biggest and baddest, and no one is allowed to forget it. Darth Vader might seem just as forceful and murderous with his imposing black helmet and heavy breathing, but Vader never goes all the way to the Dark Side. He never loses his "inner" self. Anakin Skywalker, who loves his mother and his wife, shows mercy to his long-lost son and never kills his daughter, Princess Leia. Plus, he redeems himself by killing the Emperor. For Voldemort, there is no past history of love or romance; there is no tender scene of remorse and forgiveness. Voldemort is sick and sadistic to the very end.

Fictional criminals just can't compare. Hannibal Lecter is a cannibal, but he can be captured and locked up for years, just like Grindelwald, the secondary villain in DH. Voldemort is never arrested, and the wizarding world doesn't even try to catch him. He's an evil mastermind like Sherlock Holmes's nemesis Moriarty, elusive and slippery. But Holmes is able to kill Moriarty when they plunge over a waterfall, just as John McClane is able to kill Hans Gruber in *Die Hard* by pushing him off a building. Voldemort can't be killed that easily because he's not exactly human anymore. Voldemort transplants his soul into Horcruxes to help him attain immortality. The Dark Lord multiplies himself to become invincible and to take over society and become a godlike figure, making new laws to favor the purebloods. He's more on the level of Hitler or Stalin, but with magic.

So what other fictional villains come close to Voldemort? Lex Luthor from *Superman* or the Joker from *Batman*? They all seem lightweight beside Voldemort because he is not just a comic-book baddie. He is the most complex super-villain ever created.

Verdict

Voldemort lets nothing stop him from his dastardly plans, and he strikes fear in the wizarding world with his grotesque appearance. Is he a serious contender for most diabolical character of all time? Or is he a cartoonish freak with delusions of world domination who is meant to fail? Verdict: Since Voldemort's schemes are on such a grand scale (with scales), and his sinister actions are so cold and repulsive, yes, he truly is the most evil fictional character ever.

Is Dumbledore right that Hogwarts "sorts too soon"?

Yes!

There's nothing worse for a child than being labeled at an early age, so Dumbledore is exactly right that Hogwarts sorts too soon. Dividing the students into houses at age eleven is a terrible way to run a school, since kids that age don't understand themselves too well and want to please their families and friends. It doesn't give them much room to change and grow. And the Sorting Hat seems to make a lot of mistakes, such as telling Harry in SS that he needs to be in Slytherin due to the part of Voldemort inside him. Shouldn't Harry's heroic spirit and bravery in his own soul count for more than his Slytherin traits? Also, the Sorting Ceremony seems so random and illogical. Look at Peter Pettigrew, who is placed in Gryffindor by the hat, but spends most of his cowardly life hiding behind any bully who will protect him, as we learn in PoA. He has no courage at all, and the hat should have seen that. On the opposite side, we have Regulus Black, who probably asked the Hat to put him in Slytherin to please his pureblood parents, as his brother Sirius says in OotP. But the hat makes a mistake yet again. Regulus is capable of showing compassion to his house-elf and is bold enough to hunt down and try to destroy one of Voldemort's Horcruxes [DH, p. 196]. He has a lot of courage after all, and should follow Sirius into Gryffindor instead of Slytherin. And forget about Crabbe and Goyle being even the slightest bit cunning or witty. So the Sorting System doesn't work.

What's sad is that some students ask the hat to sort them into a house based on wrong or incomplete information. Young Snape thinks Slytherin is the house of brains over brawn (it's actually Ravenclaw), and believes that his best friend Lily, a Muggle-born, will be put in that house, which is full of pureblood aristocrats. But that can't ever happen! Harry is told by Hagrid in SS that all the wizards who have gone bad are in Slytherin, which is also just not true—Sirius Black is in jail at the time, and Peter is hiding as a rat. Hermione could have been placed in Ravenclaw—the real house for brainiacs—but she tells Harry on the train in SS that she wants to follow in Dumbledore's footsteps. Would Hermione have chosen Gryffindor if she had known that Dumbledore once believed in wizarding supremacy? Probably not. The point is, there are too many outside influences on the children, which may give them the wrong idea about the Sorting System. When Ron tells his own children in the Epilogue that he will disown them if they are sorted into Slytherin, he only seems to be semi-joking, and it really isn't funny [DH, p. 755].

When Dumbledore makes the statement about Hogwarts sorting children too soon, he is talking about Snape, a Slytherin who has the courage of a Gryffindor. Snape courageously refuses to run away from Hogwarts when he knows Voldemort is returning in GoF. And Dumbledore is right about Snape's Sorting Hat experience because it ruins his whole life at eleven years old. He wants to be in the same house as his best friend Lily, but as soon as she is sorted into Gryffindor, Snape never really has a chance with her again. They are always segregated from each other with different circles of friends. She later stands in judgment of him because his housemates are Junior Death Eaters, as if he could do anything about that. And Lily loyally stands up for her friends in Gryffindor, the Marauders whom she knows are bullies and rule breakers, thinking that Snape is lying about Lupin being a werewolf. It's as if Lily loses sight of her old friend and only sees him as a product of Slytherin house, in spite of his apologies. If Snape hadn't been in Slytherin, he might not have been pulled to the Dark Side so easily by older students, such as the Malfoys and Blacks. But he could never change his house even if he wanted to because that is the Hogwarts tradition. Later, when Harry's son Albus Severus is worrying over the Sorting Ceremony, Harry assures him that even though Snape was in Slytherin, he is the bravest of all the people Harry has ever known. Yeah, right—someone should explain that to the clueless Sorting Hat, which obviously made a mistake sorting Snape. See here's the thing—people can change after age eleven. Duh!

No!

If Dumbledore really thinks the Sorting Ceremony for first years is so wrong, then why doesn't he ever try to change it? Probably because Hogwarts does *not* sort too soon, and the system works just fine. The Sorting Hat does the best it can and does not judge whether a student has a good or bad character, but what their talents are. In that respect, it's a very democratic process that looks at all the traits of someone's character without judgment. The hat gives Peter Pettigrew a chance to be in Gryffindor, and that fits since McGonagall says in PoA that he had worshipped courageous types such as James and Sirius when he was growing up. Plus, Peter has courage himself, which he proves by running around with a werewolf. It's not the fault of the Sorting Hat that Peter later uses what courage he has for bad causes—that is his choice. And the hat puts Severus and Regulus in the proper house, too, because obviously they both choose to become Death Eaters later on. Neither has the Gryffindor-style courage to stand up to their friends and change until it is almost too late.

But what about Harry—should he have been in Slytherin? There is no doubt he would have done well since Snape could have protected him a lot easier and might have favored him along with Draco. The other Slytherins would have looked up to Harry for the Parselmouth skills he discovers in CoS, which are shared with the founder of Slytherin house. But the Sorting Hat allows for free will, and people's choices make them what they are, as Dumbledore famously tells Harry in CoS. Harry asks for Gryffindor and the hat goes along with him, so that turns out just fine, too. No one in the books is ever forced into a house against their will.

Even at age eleven, kids are a mixed bag of personality traits, and the hat does its best to sort them out. Postponing the process wouldn't change that. Look at Neville Longbottom—the Sorting Hat takes a while to place him probably because he has courage like his parents, but he also has Herbology skills like a Hufflepuff. Both qualities help him later on in life, so what difference does it make which house he is in to begin with? Any smart person such as Hermione might be given a choice between Ravenclaw and some other house, because that person could excel at any subject. No one has to be an outcast just because of their house affiliation. Lily and Snape remain friends for years after entering Hogwarts, but it is Snape's bad choices that finally condemn him to be alone. The Sorting Hat is *not* to blame for all of Snape's problems.

The proof of the Sorting is in the results, and most people are exactly right for their houses. Cedric Diggory is the ultimate Hufflepuff. The Weasleys all belong in Gryffindor. Luna Lovegood has the airy wit of a true Ravenclaw. Draco can't be a more perfect Slytherin. If the System isn't broken, why change it?

Verdict

Is the Sorting System just another sign that the wizarding world's pecking order begins in childhood? Or is it just a noble tradition that has served as the bedrock of Hogwarts history going back to the Four Founders? Traditions don't have to last forever, and it would be nice if students could switch dormitories each year to see how the others lived, but alas, it never happens in the books. The houses just don't mingle enough—it's almost as if Hogwarts has its own caste system, as in India. Considering the themes of change and redemption, Dumbledore is absolutely right. Verdict: Hogwarts sorts too soon.

What is the most useful magical object for preserving history?

Magical Paintings

The living masterpieces hanging around at Hogwarts are the most useful magical objects. They aren't just wall decor, they are unique traces of real people who can speak and interact just as they did in life. They can move around between portraits in the same building and between locations if they have more than one image. So these amazing creations are so much more useful than a ghost trapped at Hogwarts or a magical photo that can't speak. Like house-elves, the paintings are somewhat limited in their movements (they have to stay inside frames for one thing), but their personalities still show through, and they have free will to speak their minds, doze off, and tell jokes.

The portraits have a job: to serve the Headmaster of Hogwarts, as the painting of ex-Headmaster Armando Dippet points out in OotP. Some paintings guard the entrances to the various houses, such as the still life paintings outside the kitchen and Hufflepuff house, and the Fat Lady and Sir Cadogan for Gryffindor house. What the paintings do for the headmaster is often serious business. When Mr. Weasley is bitten by the snake at the Ministry in OotP, Dumbledore asks one portrait named Everard to keep watch at the Ministry and sends Dilys Derwent to St. Mungo's to get information from the Healers. That's really important because time is of the essence and paintings can move back and forth much faster than people using the Floo Network. Best of all, the government cannot interfere with the portraits or track their movements, unlike living people.

The human portraits have feelings, so the Fat Lady is terrified when Sirius Black slashes her canvas with a knife in PoA. Later, the painting of Sirius Black's great-great-grandfather Phineas Nigellus tells Dumbledore he is worried the same thing might also happen to him. But Phineas is also saddened when his great-great-grandson dies and the family name of Black dies with him, which shows that these paintings can form attachments to the living.

Phineas is a unique portrait who becomes a fully developed character. He moves between the headmaster's office and Grimmauld Place in OotP, where he watches over Harry and orders him not to run away from home. So it's funny that later the portrait of Phineas is taken along when the Trio camps in DH. His role is that of a double spy—he tells the kids what is going on at Hogwarts, but he is bound to serve Headmaster Snape, so he also lets him know the whereabouts of the Trio. If not for Phineas Nigellus, Harry would never have gotten the Sword of Gryffindor in the forest because Snape wouldn't have known where to find them. No sword—no destruction of Slytherin's locket Horcrux. No sword—no deal with the goblin Griphook, and no Hufflepuff cup.

So that brings us to Dumbledore's painting behind the headmaster's chair, which has the useful task in DH of protecting the Sword of Gyrffindor in a secret compartment behind the frame. Guarding a treasure is a family tradition since his sister's portrait in Aberforth's house also hides a secret passage into Hogwarts. Without the help of Ariana's painting, the Trio could not have reunited with Neville at Hogwarts.

Not every portrait has a totally useful reason for existing. Mrs. Black's painting screams pureblood insults like a disturbed doorbell when the front door to Grimmauld Place is open in OotP, and the Fat Lady's friend Violet exists just to gossip and eat chocolate liqueurs in GoF. Sir Cadogan in PoA is annoying with his changing passwords and galloping after people in other paintings, although he is trying to be helpful. But all the portraits do one thing well—they keep the memory of the past alive better than any other magical object.

The Pensieve

The portraits at Hogwarts can't compare with the most useful object at all, which is under their noses in the headmaster's office: the Pensieve. It's not just a bowl of water, but a shimmering device that can immerse you in history with all the vivid detail of the present. Harry learns in GoF that someone can pull a silver thread of memory from their mind, swirl it into the basin, dive right in, walk around listening and learning, and then rise back out of it. The Pensieve doesn't read your mind like the Sorting Hat or rant and rave with attitude like a magical painting. It's a serious magical tool that is useful for analyzing memories. The Pensieve can reveal someone's entire life story, showing the good, the bad, and the overlooked at the time. It shows the world exactly the way it was on a day in the past, so someone may take a walk through time.

What's great about the Pensieve is that it always shows the absolute truth, without glossing over the facts. It's not like listening to a nostalgic tale colored with emotion or hearing catchphrases from an old painting. And it's not like the Mirror of Erised from SS, which only shows someone what they want to see, which might not be the truth at all. No—the Pensieve is much more like watching a video of an actual event. By splashing down into Dumbledore's memories in GoF, Harry can see the actual trials of the Death Eaters from years before. When Harry is older in OotP, he watches Madam Trelawney rise up out of the Pensieve, speaking her prophecy about the Dark Lord just as it originally happened. Through the saved-up memories of various characters, some of whom are dead, the tragic and frightening life of Tom Riddle unfolds before Harry's eyes in HBP, which helps him understand just who he is up against.

Without the useful Pensieve to clarify things, Harry would never have fully understood the friendship of his father and the other Marauders or his mother with Severus Snape that he first saw in OotP. That continues with the memories in "The Prince's Tale" in DH, which give Harry the information he needs in order to vanquish the evil in the world. They are also some of the most important scenes in the books. Harry grows up not knowing his mother, and Aunt Petunia never talks much about her except negatively. So it is a rare gift that he gets to see Lily's childhood unfold through Snape's affectionate memories. Harry is also able to understand the plans that Snape and Dumbledore made together for helping the Order of the Phoenix, such as the seven Potters and the delivery of the Sword of Gryffindor. All these memories humanize Snape in a way that Harry could never have understood otherwise, and he can trust that the Pensieve is showing the truth, uncolored by emotions or misunderstandings. There's just no other way he could have discovered his destiny, which is to sacrifice himself for the good of all. Therefore, the Pensieve is the key Harry needed to gain the courage to go back and face Voldemort, making it the most useful object in the series.

Verdict

If a picture is worth a thousand words, then magical paintings that communicate are priceless. If memories are golden, then the ones swirling around in the Pensieve are a treasure trove. Harry needs both the paintings and the Pensieve to complete his task, but from one of them he receives a bounty of rare and helpful information. Verdict: The Pensieve is the most useful magical object.

Are the female characters too stereotyped?

Yes!

The girls and women in Harry Potter are all stereotyped, and there's just no excuse for it. Young witches study hard at Hogwarts apparently so they can marry immediately and have as many children as possible. Even the strongest female characters seem to plan their whole futures around their boyfriends. Molly Weasley has no life beyond the Burrow. Hermione is fixated on Ron. Fleur lives just for Bill. Tonks is so determined to marry Remus Lupin that she throws her life away. Harry's mother Lily existed just to be . . . well, Harry's mother and James's wife. What did she want to study after Hogwarts? What was her career going to be? None of that ever comes up. The career women are sometimes evil, like Umbridge or Rita Skeeter, or depressed, like Tonks and Trelawney, or old and alone, like Minerva McGonagall and Bathilda Bagshot. None of them have well-balanced lives. None of them have the maturity, wisdom, and power of Dumbledore, and that's a shame. The men, good and bad, run the wizarding world.

Girls and women are portrayed as overwhelmed by their emotions and that limits their choices in life. Except for the serene Luna Lovegood, the females react to every little thing by either blowing up in anger or falling to the floor sobbing uncontrollably. Merope Riddle gives up and dies because her husband left her. Cho Chang is so weepy over Cedric's death that Harry has to stop dating her. Madame Trelawney is an alcoholic, just like Winky, the only female house-elf. Narcissa Malfoy has Lady in Distress syndrome: With her husband in prison and a son controlled by Voldemort, she sees no option but to run and ask a man for help. Only Severus Snape can solve her problem, and he has to give in when she cries, begs, spills wine, and acts like a helpless female [HBP, p. 33]. Plus, she resorts to trickery with the Unbreakable Vow. So she is both weak and dishonest.

Real women have to be controlling nags. Molly Weasley scolds her husband, Arthur, as if he is one of the children, and she isn't afraid to give Sirius Black a tongue-lashing about parenting Harry in OotP. All it does is make Molly sound like a petty shrew. Her younger version, Hermione, takes it as her mission in life to give Harry and Ron a stern lecture every day. Not that they listen to her very much, but it lets her feel useful. Mrs. Black's portrait in OotP is the best nag in the books—she is still screeching from the walls of home long after her death. Thanks, Mom.

Of course, the real "hero" of Harry Potter is a male, so the females only exist to be "helpers" along the way. Ginny and Cho are just there as love objects for Harry, while Luna is the jester who makes him laugh. Hermione is his personal encyclopedia, but she is also talented at packing her giant pocketbook for extended camping. In DH, all of Hermione's intelligence goes to waste while she sits around a tent, crying about Ron and drying off wet clothing. Then there are the Real house-witches of Potter County: Molly Weasley cooks, folds socks, and knits sweaters, while Petunia Dursley scrubs the kitchen night after night. They might as well be house-elves. Of course, Harry is forced to work in the Dursley household, and Molly makes all the boys and men clean up Grimmauld Place, but the message is that women are drudges who think up boring work and ruin the fun for everybody else.

Ginny Weasley's role is the most stereotyped of all. Not only is she the perfect fairy-tale princess in love with the hero, but she has to have special protection in *Deathly Hallows*. She is locked up safely at home, and then at Hogwarts in the Room of Requirement where Harry tells her to "keep out of the way, keep safe" [DH, p. 627]. And this is the girl who is supposed to be so bold and outspoken, the queen of the Bat-Bogey Hex? Harry later releases her from the Room of Requirement and she is glad to join the fight, but in the end, her mother has to save her. It's great that Molly actually fights a duel with Bellatrix Lestrange, and she is one of the few women to get some satisfaction in battle, but why is it that Ginny is treated like a fragile doll who suddenly can't stand up for herself? Why doesn't she get to be heroic just like Neville or Ron? Simple—this is the sexist world of Harry Potter, and she's a girl.

No!

No way—magic makes everyone equal and gives women their own special power. Girls get exactly the same education at Hogwarts, have the same opportunities to fly around and play Quidditch, and are offered the same career goals after leaving school. No matter what happens to Nymphadora Tonks later in life, the fact remains that she studied for years to be an Auror, and in OotP, she is the equal of Moody and Shacklebolt. Minerva McGonagall is a teacher at Hogwarts, head of Gryffindor house, a tough Deputy Headmistress, and then takes over as head of the school after Dumbledore dies, so she is one of the most successful women in the books. Umbridge isn't the only woman who works her way up in government—what about Mafalda Hopkirk, Griselda Marchbanks, and Amelia Bones? Hogwarts does not have a male doctor, but a Nurse-Healer: Madam Pomfrey. The wizarding world does not discriminate against women in any way.

The girls who are Harry's age never take a back seat to him, and they are certainly not stereotypes. Luna isn't just a whacko—she speaks the truth in HBP even when it makes Harry uncomfortable. Cho Chang talks a lot about her late boyfriend Cedric's death in OotP, which might not be romantic, but it is probably good for Harry to discuss since he watches Cedric die and then has nightmares about it. Hermione is the fast thinker who can solve a logic riddle, Apparate them all out of danger, and still have time for some heavy reading before bedtime. How can anyone call her a stereotype when she does so many surprising and innovative things? Hermione saves Harry's life dozens of times! And finally, there is the vivacious and wonderful Ginny Weasley—no one would accuse her of having less power than Harry or her brothers. When Harry leaves her behind to go fight, it's not to protect her because she's a girl—it's to protect her because he's in love with her and can't bear to see her get hurt.

If the girls and women are emotional, well, so are the boys and men. Harry is often upset and lovesick, too, and everyone in the books likes to shout and fuss sometimes. The women are just passionate about the people they love, so what's wrong with that? How is Hermione obsessing about Ron any different than Harry being in love with Ginny and watching her dot move around on the Marauder's Map when he's camping out in DH? It's true that Tonks is sometimes depressed, but so is Sirius Black in OotP when he sulks in his room, which Harry also does at Grimmauld Place. Funny thing is, it's the girls, Hermione and Ginny, who convince Harry to cheer up and stop being so depressed. And remember—Tonks keeps working as an Auror and Member of the Order the whole time she is having problems, and in DH she defies the Dark Lord in a major way by marrying a werewolf. She rocks!

MuggleNet.com's Harry Potter Should Have Died

Mrs. Weasley runs a huge household with more children than any other family in the books and still works for Dumbledore and the Order of the Phoenix. She is a blood traitor and her whole family is always in mortal danger. She doesn't let anything stop her, and as her blazing duel with Bellatrix Lestrange proves: She's fierce! It's true that all people marry at a younger age in the wizarding world, women and men, and they have old-fashioned values. The family is the most important social group in their society. Women don't just become mothers, they become teachers who homeschool their kids until they go to Hogwarts. Caring for magical children takes a lot of stamina and imagination. Look what Molly goes through with the twins: It's not just simple babysitting, it is more like herding cats. As the tale of Tom Riddle proves, a good family and mother can keep a boy from being abandoned by society. Thank goodness Neville has his gran to raise him, and Teddy Lupin has his own grandmother, Andromeda. Harry is an orphan, but his mother's blood protects him from Voldemort long after her death.

Most of the women in the books are totally unique. When Madam Trelawney hurls crystal balls at the Death Eaters in DH it is not a stereotype. Neither is Madam Pince in the library with her book of jinxes in *Quidditch Through the Ages*, Mrs. Figg standing up to Dementors in OotP, or Bertha Jorkins confronting Barty Crouch over his crimes in GoF. Harry couldn't have defeated Voldemort without Narcissa Malfoy, who chooses *on her own* to defy the Dark Lord so she can see Draco again. Just like Lily Potter, she has motherly love that is stronger than Voldemort's evil, and it saves Harry's life again. Women have the power the Dark Lord knows not.

Verdict

Are the women in Harry Potter doomed to lives of second-class companionship, continuous motherhood, and unhappy spinsterhood? Or are the witches creative and strong, fully equal to the wizards? It's true the wizarding world is old-fashioned, but there are plenty of witches in the books who are full of vibrant girl-power. No matter how you look at it, any book that features the always smart, always brave Hermione Granger as the main female lead is not one that paints a stereotypical picture of women. Verdict: No, the females are not too stereotyped.

Is the final duel between Harry and Voldemort a disappointment?

Yes!

The so-called duel between Harry and Voldemort in DH was a big zero. It really wasn't even a duel, but a long, long conversation about love and loyalty, Snape and Lily, the Elder Wand and Draco, droning on and on with almost no action. Harry knows he is supposed to kill Voldemort, not just disarm him, so how the heck does he know that *Expelliarmus* will backfire and kill the Dark Lord? It's not convincing that Harry even completely understands the Elder Wand's special powers at that point, so he couldn't really know what was going to happen. Was it just the Elder Wand's allegiance for Harry that killed the Dark Lord, or was Voldemort's soul splintered so much that it just flew out of his body? It's mind-numbing to try to figure it out, and there shouldn't be so many questions about a duel that was supposed to be definitive and clear.

Fans have been looking forward to the final duel ever since the end of OotP when the prophecy was explained to Harry. Obviously, one of them had to be killed by the other, so we knew there would be a fight to the death and only one of them would be the last wizard standing. This duel was supposed to be the grande finale, the high noon of duels with all sorts of made-for-Sports-Center moments. It was supposed to be Harry versus Voldemort in the arena, in the spotlight, face-to-face with no one else to help and nowhere to hide. This was *it*—the Big Smackdown—time for Harry to put Voldie in his place and show all that he had learned in seven years at Hogwarts.

Instead, Harry mutters one spell—the boring Disarming Charm—and splat: Voldemort falls without a whimper. In the book, the word mundane is used to describe it, because even J.K.R. must have realized that as duels go, this one was full of blah. The sun comes up; the Dark Lord falls down. Not much there to write home about, and the other characters were probably standing around thinking "Huh?" It is a wasted moment and the anticlimax of all time. Of course fans were disappointed—J.K.R. truly let us down with this one.

No!

So what if it isn't an action-packed duel—Harry bravely faces the most evil wizard of all time and zaps him out of existence. And, *of course*, there is a lot of talk. This is Harry's big chance to honor what he has seen in Snape's memories, and that's the big payoff, not some long violent duel with blood and gore. Harry lets Voldemort know that someone has fooled him for years—zing! What could be more damaging to a villain's big ego? The final duel couldn't be just bloody revenge for all the deaths, because that would drag Harry down to the level of a Death Eater. In the end, Harry acts in a way that would make Dumbledore proud—he gives Voldemort a last chance to express some remorse, showing mercy and proving he is the better man [DH, p. 741].

And it's awesome and right that Harry uses *Expelliarmus* to kill Voldemort instead of *Avada Kedavra*. He uses a charm instead of a curse and a defensive spell instead of an Unforgivable Curse. Harry doesn't need to use something complicated or to waste his time and energy throwing Stunners and making fireworks. Enough fighting already! Harry knows that Voldemort is going to try one spell only—*Avada Kedavra*—because he wants Harry gone in a flash. But the Elder Wand recognizes Harry as the true owner and when he shouts *Expelliarmus*, Voldemort's own *Avada* curse rebounds on him. It's simple, elegant, and gets rid of the Dark Lord forever. It's extremely satisfying and anything else would have been almost inappropriate.

Verdict

Fans expected the duel at the end of DH to be like a shoot-out in the Old West. Instead, it is more like a talk-show interview with a deadly ending. While many fans can admire Harry's restraint and his compassion for the psycho who killed his parents, most people were expecting the hero to kick Voldemort's butt for his evil deeds. Since Voldemort mainly gets off with a lecture about love, the verdict has to be that the final duel fails to live up to some (admittedly) very high expectations.

Who would win in a fight: Dumbledore or Gandalf?

Gandalf

Gandalf from *Lord of the Rings* would win a fight against Dumbledore, hands down. Dumbledore has no will power, and in HBP, he fries his own hand to a blackened claw by trying on the Horcrux ring. But look at Gandalf—he isn't even tempted by the Ring of Power and never puts it on. Dumbledore is so pitiful in HBP after drinking the poisonous potion in the Horcrux cave that the old guy can't fight Draco on the tower. But Gandalf slugs it out with the giant Balrog Fire Demon for weeks without help of any kind. There's just no contest there.

Dumbledore can never seem to do the one thing that matters—protect a bunch of little kids from the Dark Lord. Half the time, he doesn't even know what is going on at Hogwarts, so what good is all that alleged superior intelligence? He has one good duel in the whole series—"The Only One He Ever Feared" in OotP—and really Harry wins that for him and frightens Voldemort away. Even in the afterlife, like we see in DH, Dumbledore is just a sad old man sitting around in a train station, and his life story is as full of flaws as any Muggle's. How different from Gandalf, who roars back from death into Middle Earth to save the hobbits and men. None of the other characters, including the elves, would have had a clue without him. Plus, he can still ride his horse Shadowfax like a knight to the rescue. *Dumbledore shall not pass!*

Dumbledore

But wait—according to OotP, Dumbledore is the only wizard the Dark Lord ever feared, right? Did Sauron and his evil minions ever really fear Gandalf? No way—Sauron just goes on building up his Orc Army and watching people with his Eye, and there isn't a thing Gandalf can do about it. Plus Sauron uses his warlord sidekick, Saruman, to kick Gandalf around like a hacky-sack. Kings Theoden and Denethor have no respect for Gandalf and make up foolish names about him like "Stormcrow" or "Greyhaim." Even the hobbits disobey him continuously. Dumbledore has a lot more power over people than Gandalf, which is obvious because they love and respect Dumbledore. And with the Elder Wand, he is nearly superhuman, so he can sweep up the floor with Gandalf and his old wooden staff!

Dumbledore is always in demand with the Wizengamot, the Minister of Magic, and Hogwarts because he basically knows everything about everything in the wizarding world. Gandalf is never sure of himself and is always riding off to visit the Gondor scroll library to remind him of things he has forgotten about, such as the Ring of Power. How does he forget that?

Voldemort never comes close to killing Dumbledore, and Harry learns in SS that Dumbledore vanquished the racist Grindelwald, saving Europe and ending WWII in 1945. That is so completely different from Gandalf wrestling the Balrog in some distant cave and then turning up confused in Fangorn Forest, which was just a waste of time during a war when people needed his help. The Fellowship of the Ring should never have gone under the mountain anyway, and that is Gandalf's bad call, which nearly gets them all killed.

In HBP, Dumbledore grows ill and bravely asks Snape to finish him off at the right time. What's wrong with that? The whole point of the HP series is that immortality does not help anybody. Dumbledore thinks death is a great adventure and it doesn't frighten him, but Gandalf shakes like a fraidy-cat in the Mines of Moria, thinking the Balrog might rise up to get him.

In HBP, Dumbledore has already lost his hand, but he is able to swim right into the Horcrux cave, drink the poison, and fend off the Inferi. Then he flies home on a broom, faces his enemies, saves Harry and Draco, and dies with dignity. Nothing Gandalf ever does in battle can match what Dumbledore does in that one night. We have only seen a fraction of the magic both wizards are capable of, but one of them lives in a world with magic in it and the other lives in the wizarding world, which includes non-magical areas, too. Gandalf is a big fish in a small pond. In a duel between Dumbledore and Gandalf, Dumbledore would open up a can and show Gandalf how it's done in the big leagues.

Verdict

So, who would win the fight? Both Gandalf and Dumbledore can be fierce and impressive in battle. It's true one of them dies an old man, while the other defies death and lives. But Obi-Wan Kenobi dies in Star Wars, *and he still helps Luke clown the Empire. Verdict: Dumbledore would put the* wn *in* pwn.

Should J.K.R. write an eighth book about the next generation?

Yes!

J.K.R. should write an eighth book—and more beyond that. The Epilogue of *Deathly Hallows* sets the stage perfectly with the introduction of young James, Albus Severus, and Lily Potter, plus Hugo and Rose Weasley, and Scorpius Malfoy. Every reader wants to follow them to Hogwarts and the Sorting Ceremony, which could be full of surprises. Imagine the reversals if Albus Severus is actually put in Slytherin, while Scorpius is put in Gryffindor. Or what if they are both put in the same house and have to be roommates? Fans love to speculate about this, but J.K.R. is the one who should have the last word. If she doesn't, there is no doubt that fan-fiction writers will take over the story for the next hundred years.

Another good reason for J.K.R. to write the book is that there are so many unresolved issues in the series. What becomes of S.P.E.W. and the rights of house-elves? Were the Malfoys changed forever by the death of Voldemort? And is there some new force of evil lurking about in the halls of Hogwarts? Please, J.K.R., keep on writing, and we promise to read every word. Twenty times!

No!

No way—J.K.R. should just leave it alone and go write something else. Her original plan was to stop at seven books, and that was a good idea. All good things must come to an end, and Jo performed a miraculous feat by delivering seven extremely long books without the story deteriorating. It's better to go out on top like *Seinfeld* than to create a less-than-amazing sequel, like we've seen from the *American Pie* and *National Lampoon* movies. J.K.R. has cemented a place in literary history. Does she want to be remembered only as the woman who invented "that wizard kid with glasses"? Or, does she want to be taken seriously as a versatile writer who can do so much more in other genres besides heroic fantasy?

As both a billionaire and the richest woman in the UK, J.K.R. is in a position to basically do whatever she wants. And she doesn't want to write an eighth book, so it would be selfish of fans to demand she continue writing.

Verdict

Should J.K.R. give the fans what they want—more, more, more? Or is it better to leave the barrier at Platform 9 and 3/4 closed for good? Of course, new readers will also keep coming along, and some older fans will never let it go—the bottom line is that J.K.R. will be able to sell books regardless of what she writes about. As much as we would selfishly love to continue reading new wizarding world adventures, we understand that J.K.R. has probably had enough. Verdict: All good things must come to an end.

Would the series be stronger if Voldemort had killed Harry?

Yes!

The ending of the series would be much more powerful if Harry had actually died for his friends at the hand of Voldemort. Instead, Harry "fake dies" and comes back to life, and after that the whole story seems like an anticlimactic cheat. Magic is *not* supposed to keep someone from dying the way it does with Harry. J.K.R. wrote that as a definitive statement on her website, then broke her own rule. But aren't Horcruxes magic? Isn't the Elder Wand magic? Isn't Lily's sacrificial blood that runs in Harry's veins magic? All those things help Harry stay alive. And what about Dumbledore telling Harry in SS that Nicholas Flamel and his wife aren't afraid of death and that it's a big adventure no one should fear? Yet Harry dies and comes back to life at Dumbledore's suggestion in the "King's Cross" chapter. In DH, Harry is only semi-dead for what seems like a split second (which may be just a dream) and then he doesn't really fight Voldemort at all, but preaches him a sermon about love and remorse. What a crock! So is Harry ever in danger at all? No. Is Voldemort really that powerful at all? No. It just seems lame and unsatisfying. What does Harry really give up in order to win? Nothing. He can't die anyway, so there is no sacrifice.

Many other characters die fighting for Harry, and that is meaningful because they can't cheat death the way he does. Even Voldemort taunts him in DH for letting all his friends die while he lives, and that's a valid point. Harry hardly gets a scratch at the Battle of Hogwarts, dead or not. And according to the Epilogue, Harry's big reward is that he gets to lead a ho-hum suburban life with Ginny and the kids. That was his big reward for staying alive? Where is the drama in that for the fans? It would be much more heroic to die on the battlefield and throw away the happy life he could have had. If Voldemort and Harry had *both* died, ending the war between them and saving the wizarding world, it would be a much stronger finish to the series.

No!

No way—the story is perfect just as it ends, with Harry victorious and Voldemort dead. Harry has suffered enough, and he needs to get Voldemort out of his head so he can be normal. Suffering and dying won't avenge the deaths of all his friends or bring them back. This way, he chooses to give up his life just as his mother did, providing protection for everyone he loves, which miraculously lets him live. His parents would have wanted that, and so would Sirius, Dumbledore, Lupin, Tonks, and even Snape. The ending is completely satisfying because he really does die, but he rises again like the phoenix because his soul is pure. Then Harry has the satisfaction of telling Voldemort about the brilliant plans of Dumbledore and Snape, who completely fooled him for years. That is the best revenge for their deaths.

The message is that coming so close to dying, Harry learns to be compassionate to everyone and value a simple life with his wife and kids. If he had truly died and was cheated out of that happiness, what good would it do? He deserves to live and be happy after struggling for years. If Voldemort had killed him dead, as he had so many others, what would that prove?

Imagine you're J.K.R. riding on a train when the idea for Harry Potter comes to you. All the sudden, you get a flash of inspiration—the greatest story ever told. You're so excited you can hardly stand it. Yes—you're going to write a story. It's about a boy whose life *completely sucks*. And then he dies.

And besides all that—what would the fans think if Harry died? Most of them would be grief-stricken and horrified. The message that evil could triumph over love would make everyone feel cheated. If readers cried after the deaths of Hedwig and Dobby, just imagine if they could see no future for Harry, who was much too young to die. Would fans today want to encourage their future children to read such a long series only to be disappointed? Also, that $300 million theme park in Orlando, Florida, would be kind of depressing if Harry died. "Hey, let's go walk around this guy's grave!"

Verdict

Harry is able to dodge death and become The Man Who Lived. Is this an ending that cheats readers who expect Harry to be the sacrificial Man Who Died? The blood protection and Elder Wand both save Harry, and fans love that Harry becomes the Man Who Kinda Lived Twice. The complexity of that is better than if Voldemort had merely killed him dead. Verdict: No—the series would not be stronger if Harry had been killed.

Is Severus Snape a hero?

No!

There can only be one true hero in the seven-part series, and that is Harry Potter because he always tries to do the right thing. Snape can never be a hero because he has too many flaws and is always nasty and mostly out for himself. According to Dumbledore in HBP, Snape is the reason Harry's parents are hunted down and killed in the first place, because Snape overhears a prophecy about the birth of a child who will be the Dark Lord's equal. Snape can't wait to run to tell Voldemort, and he doesn't mind that it is all about killing a baby until he finds out it is the child of his old friend Lily Potter. His so-called love for Lily is creepy and obsessive, since she is already married to James. What Snape really wants is for Voldemort to get rid of James so Snape can have Lily to himself! That's despicable and proves that he can never be a hero. Sure, he puts on a show for Dumbledore about trying to save Harry for Lily's sake, but Snape never cares about Harry at all as a person. And it's self-serving that Snape gets a cushy job at Hogwarts in return for pretending to care.

Snape is put in the right house because he is a true Slytherin just like Voldemort—not some noble character. Look at his teaching style, which is sadistic—there is nothing brave about bullying young children for fun or punishing them for their parents' perceived misdeeds. It demonstrates a lack of emotional maturity. There is no heroism in making Neville and Harry feel stupid, as Snape does from the first day of Potions class in SS. No good guy would taunt Hermione—a passionate, dedicated student—about her overgrown teeth when she is already crying, as dear Professor Snape does in GoF.

Snape cares little for the consequences of what he says and does. Snape taunts Sirius Black in OotP about hiding from Voldemort just enough to push his buttons, and Snape knowingly sends him to his death at the Department of Mysteries. And in PoA, he despicably outs Lupin as a werewolf so Lupin loses the only good job he ever had, his teaching job at Hogwarts.

Then Lupin turns into a social outcast. In HBP, after Snape knows that Dumbledore is already weakened and has only a year to live, he lets Narcissa make an Unbreakable Vow with him that forces him to kill Dumbledore. And all along, Snape barely does enough to help Harry and is always malicious and petty. He is insulting and impatient when he tries to teach Occlumency in OotP, so Harry never learns to do it properly, which puts his life in danger. In DH, Snape takes the Sword of Gryffindor to the Forest of Dean, but he makes things so difficult that Harry nearly freezes to death and drowns. As Headmaster of Hogwarts in DH, Snape is nothing like Dumbledore because he allows the Carrows to torture children, even some of Harry's best friends. Doesn't that prove what a horrible coward he is? He can't stand up to the other Death Eaters or to the other teachers. He deserves to be killed and eaten by Nagini. J.K.R. said it plainly herself shortly after DH was released—"Snape is vindictive. He's cruel. He's not a big man" [JKR-MTV].

Yes!

No matter what J.K.R. says, Severus Snape is second only to Harry as a hero for millions of fans. In spite of his stern appearance and his supposed connections to the Dark Side, he always tries to do the right thing. Yes, he takes a wrong turn as a boy and becomes a Death Eater, but he changes. That is his heroic message—people can redeem themselves. As seen through a memory in DH, Snape realizes his huge mistake in telling Voldemort the prophecy about Harry and vows to do whatever he can to save Lily's family, including James and the baby. That is bravery personified and Snape receives nothing in return for helping the Order of the Phoenix except for a thankless job teaching Potions at Hogwarts. Voldemort only gives Lily a chance to live at all because Snape asks him to spare her—another brave request that ends up keeping Harry alive when his mother sacrifices her life instead of stepping aside. Without Snape, Harry would have been toast.

Snape has two choices—he can waste away from grief, or he can help watch over Harry in case Voldemort returns. It would have been easy for Snape to walk away from that responsibility. Harry isn't his son and only reminds Snape of everything he has missed out on in life since James married Lily. But Snape is tough and heroically takes a much harder path and stays at Hogwarts. He keeps up friendships with the Malfoys and other Death Eaters so that when the Dark Lord rises again he can say he has been loyal all along. That is why he is prepared to return to Voldemort at the graveyard in GoF, which is just as brave as anything Harry ever does. Snape's only motivation in life is to save Lily's son, and he has to carefully hide his true feelings for years with Occlumency so no one will find out. The Dark Lord could have caught him lying and killed him at any time. Who knows how many ways Snape was punished over the years, physically and mentally? No wonder he feels that Harry doesn't appreciate anything he does, because Harry never thinks of Snape as brave or heroic until after he dies.

Snape is a hero who never gives up and never runs away, and that takes guts. He is Dumbledore's most trusted friend. He protects the secrets of the Order of the Phoenix, and in DH saves the lives of Lupin and George Weasley. Also in DH, Harry sees one of Snape's memories about the Yule Ball, when Snape and Dumbledore are talking about how cowardly Igor Karkaroff is, and Dumbledore implies that Snape is heroic enough to be in Gryffindor, so it's a mystery why J.K.R. would dispute what she wrote herself in the book. Harry says plainly in the Epilogue that Snape was braver than anyone he had ever known. That's right—*anyone*. So whether fans love Snape or hate him, he is a hero in Harry's eyes.

Verdict

Is Snape just a coward who serves two masters? Or is Snape a true hero who protects Harry for the most noble reasons? What should matter more: the snarky Slytherin things he says or his Gryffindor-style willingness to save people? Harry names his youngest son after Severus and tells him that Snape had courage, and that's a big deal. Verdict: Snape is a hero of the series, too.

Is S.P.E.W. good or bad for house-elves?

Good

S.P.E.W. can only be a good thing for the house-elves because someone needs to help them—even if they're too brainwashed to know it. Hermione starts the Society for the Promotion of Elfish Welfare in GoF because she believes passionately that house-elves deserve to have the same rights as humans. House-elves are slaves with Stockholm syndrome, plain and simple. Just because they have been slaves for centuries doesn't justify their continued enslavement. Remember the creepy elf heads mounted on the wall at Grimmauld Place in OotP? That's barbaric, and someone has to stop that madness from happening in future generations.

Unfortunately, Hermione goes about things the wrong way in OotP when she knits hundreds of little hats and leaves them around the castle. This plan to free the house-elves of Hogwarts backfires and infuriates everyone. She is trying to establish equal rights for the house-elves, but she doesn't see that the house-elves aren't ready for such a change.

Hermione achieves greater success with her pro-elf mission by simply talking to people than by trying to manipulate the elves to free themselves. She convinces Harry to have sympathy for Kreacher, who has a hand in Sirius Black's death. Harry takes Hermione's advice and believes that Kreacher is a victim of cruel circumstances. Instead of having him thrown into Azkaban, Harry takes Kreacher on as his new servant. That is the real key to S.P.E.W.: to treat house-elves with understanding. While her initial plan doesn't work, Hermione has one thing right: With good treatment over time, perhaps house-elves can be retaught to live independent lives—they just need to get used to the idea. Revolutions don't really happen overnight.

Bad

Hermione has the best intentions, but she completely misunderstands the very house-elves she is committed to freeing. Not only does Hermione make an idiot of herself when she forces Harry, Ron, and Neville to join her schoolgirl crusade, but there are major flaws in her plan. For one thing, the elves at Hogwarts don't belong to Hermione, so how can she free them? No matter how much knitting she puts around the Common Room, she has no jurisdiction over those elves. Hermione is completely ignorant about house-elves and their lives until she lives at Grimmauld Place in OotP, and it shows. She is a Muggle-born who has never seen an elf until she meets Dobby and Winky, and then suddenly she thinks she is an expert. Hermione arrogantly refuses to listen to the chorus of voices urging her to drop the issue—she writes off their protests as the predictable resistance to change every revolutionary must overcome.

House-elves have carved out a cozy mutually beneficial existence for themselves, not altogether different from the relationship between dogs and their owners. Dogs provide unconditional love and loyalty, and their owners respond by providing them life's essentials. And so it is with the house-elves, who cook and clean for their owners and in return receive safety, food, and shelter. The house-elves are happy with this relationship and their place in society.

Verdict

There's no doubt that Hermione means well when she tries to railroad the house-elves into a new way of life. She does, however, stubbornly ignore the elves' wishes and she fails to appreciate the beauty in the relationships they have with humans. Her inability to listen to conflicting evidence stand in the way of her understanding and result in her personal shock when the elves aren't grateful for being pushed aboard the Freedom Train. Verdict: No, S.P.E.W. was not good for the house-elves.

Which character is more underestimated by others: Kreacher or Peter Pettigrew?

Kreacher

House-elves don't get much respect in the wizarding world, so it's not surprising that bat-eared old Kreacher, the family servant from Grimmauld Place, would be the most underestimated character. Maybe it's the fact that he has a creepy lair under the boiler at Grimmauld Place in OotP and walks around muttering racist slurs as if he has elf-dementia. For whatever the reason, people expect nothing from him, but Kreacher is full of surprises, bad and good.

Sirius Black treats Kreacher with contempt because the elf reminds him of his unhappy family life, and in return, Kreacher hates Sirius for breaking Mrs. Black's heart (if that was really possible). Yet Sirius takes it totally for granted that Kreacher will stay loyal, even when he foolishly orders him out of the house. That is a huge mistake, because Kreacher takes the opportunity to run away and get revenge, giving the Malfoys information that helps lure Sirius to his death at the Department of Mysteries. It's a spectacular plot twist because the other characters, as well as the readers, never really suspect that Kreacher will be very important to the plot. He seems to be just another eccentric elf lost in his own little world. Later in DH, Harry has to admit that Sirius treated Kreacher in a terrible and indifferent manner, overlooking the warning signs on the way to disaster.

When Harry inherits Kreacher along with Sirius's house and becomes his new master, he tries to treat Kreacher with more understanding. Sirius never thought about asking Kreacher questions, but in DH, Harry orders the elf to talk, and learns that he actually helped Regulus Black steal a Horcrux from Voldemort. Who would expect a story like that from Kreacher? And the reason the old elf is always so upset over the death of Mrs. Black is that he feels guilty over the loss of her son, whose corpse Kreacher had to leave behind in the Inferi Cave. So Kreacher has been suffering over that for years and Sirius never understood. If only Sirius hadn't been so wrapped up in his own problems, he might have talked to Kreacher and found out the truth. Instead, Sirius seals his own fate by underestimating a house-elf's free will and cunning, plus believing that mistreatment of house-elves doesn't have consequences.

Voldemort makes the same mistake. He leaves Kreacher to die in the Horcrux cave, never realizing that house-elves have powers that wizards don't have. Unlike a human wizard who would have been trapped, Kreacher is able to Disapparate out of there and survive. Good thing, too, because without Kreacher, Harry couldn't have gotten the Horcrux locket back from Mundungus Fletcher so it could be destroyed in DH.

Kreacher is much more complex than he seems. It turns out he was never as feeble and incompetent as Sirius thought, and he was also not as mean and horrible as Harry (and many readers) believed. Regulus is the only one who really cares about him, and Kreacher loves him in return. Yes, he could love, and he also grows as a character. In the end, he accepts Harry as his new master—learning to respect a half-blood. And then he leads the house-elves into the fight during the Battle of Hogwarts in DH. So Kreacher actually redeems himself by the end of the series, and who would have thought that could happen? Never underestimate a house-elf.

Peter Pettigrew

Even more than Kreacher, Peter Pettigrew is the outwardly pathetic character who is overlooked and underestimated. From the time Peter is just a boy, people have low expectations of him. Professor McGonagall says in PoA that she felt sorry for him, and his best friends felt they had to help him all the time because he wasn't as talented, as Sirius Black says in the Shrieking Shack. But Peter was never really that much of a loser. After all, just like the other Marauders, he learns to become an Animagus, able to transform himself into an animal, which is advanced and quasi-legal magic. And even though his animal form—a rat—is smaller than that of James or Sirius, Peter isn't afraid to run around with a werewolf, either. So he's just as tough as James and Sirius, but they dismiss him as if they are superior, and underestimate his abilities, which is a big mistake.

After they leave school, the Potters and Sirius take Peter's loyalty for granted, but by then Peter is obviously looking out for himself. As Sirius explains in the Shrieking Shack in PoA, Peter unexpectedly gets a chance to betray the Potters and serve Lord Voldemort when he becomes the trusted Secret-Keeper of Godric's Hollow. So, the Potters are killed by Voldemort, then Sirius goes after Peter for revenge, which should be easy, right? After all, Peter is just little Wormtail and Sirius is the stronger wizard, full of righteous anger. But Sirius totally underestimates the situation. Peter blows up the street, kills a bunch of Muggles, cuts off his own finger for proof of death, and gets Sirius thrown into Azkaban for twelve years.

In doing all that, Peter nearly pulls off the perfect crime and no one ever suspects him. Lupin, Sirius, Dumbledore, Fudge, and McGonagall believe Peter is dead, as does the rest of the world. No one bothers to check the old rat at the Burrow who is living with the Weasley family. Yep—the underestimated Peter is also Scabbers, Ron's pet in the first three books. All that would be amazing enough for a character no one believes is capable of anything, but Peter has even more tricks up his sleeve. Harry shows him mercy in PoA, and then immediately Peter escapes and runs off to find Voldemort. When we next see him in GoF, Voldemort is ordering him to milk the giant snake Nagini of her venom—risky business for a rat Animagus, and undeniably brave for an alleged coward. By the time he cuts off his own hand to bring the Dark Lord back to life at the end of GoF, no one in the wizarding world is underestimating him anymore.

Even people who have read the books several times still think of him as Little Peter Pettigrew, the hapless and helpless Marauder. You have to do the math to see the truth about Peter: He kills twelve Muggles, plus Cedric Diggory and Frank Bryce with Voldemort's wand, and betrays Bertha Jorkins and the two Potters, for a total of seventeen victims (and Harry in the graveyard was nearly one of those victims). In "Snape's Worst Memory" in OotP, Peter obviously enjoys watching a schoolmate being taunted and bullied, and that was his true self all along. But even those closest to Peter refused to see that dark side of his character until it was too late. They underestimated him at their own peril.

Verdict

Kreacher is under the radar as a house-elf, and no one suspects how bad (or good) he can be. Peter Pettigrew takes advantage of his friends' naïve trust and double-

crosses them big-time, then hides as a rat for twelve years, fooling even Dumbledore. Kreacher at least shows predictability in his loyalty to the House of Black, but Peter, on the other hand, literally blows people away several times with his hidden agendas. While Kreacher grows and changes through the books, Peter is always the same; he shouldn't have been such a mystery to those around him. Verdict: Because Kreacher plays a much larger role than anyone ever expected in a million years, he is the most underestimated character.

Which movie deserves the most credit for setting a new standard?

A few movies in the series seem to have just a little more heart than the others and remind us why we enjoy reading the books so much. That's the case with these two films.

Harry Potter and the Prisoner of Azkaban

The unique style of director Alfonso Cuaron makes *Prisoner of Azkaban* the best movie in the series and the film that sets a Galleon standard for HP movies to come. It is quirky and artistic, full of dark details and textures that are true to the magic of the books. From the Dursleys' suburban home to the natural world of northern Scotland, everything feels authentic. Everyone wears hand-knits that seem to come right off Molly Weasley's knitting needles. The exquisite paintings at Hogwarts seem to double in number and really come to life. The Knight Bus is off-kilter and madcap, while the Leaky Cauldron seems full of antique atmosphere. The hippogriff takes flight and soars over a sparkling lake, while the *Monster Book of Monsters* lurks under the bed. From the candy-filled shelves at Honeydukes to the Teacup Tower in Madam Trelawney's classroom, this movie is a feast for the eyes. Oh—and don't forget the Marauder's Map, the Boggarts, the Dementors, a shrunken head, Flying Aunt Marge, and the Grim. And unlike *Order of the Phoenix*, PoA has a Quidditch match—in the rain.

With such a bounty of special effects, it's amazing that so much character development happens, but that's part of the depth of this movie. Harry is older and dealing with issues of life and death, sadness and anger. Ron and Hermione are starting to flirt and spend time together. Draco and his gang are becoming nastier than ever and causing trouble. There is a menagerie of wayward pets: Scabbers, Crookshanks, Buckbeak, and Padfoot. And, of course, for the first time we see Gary Oldman as Sirius Black, godfather and prison escapee, and David Thewlis as Professor Lupin, a man with many secrets. Michael Gambon becomes the new Dumbledore, playing the role with more energy and vigor than the frail Richard Harris could muster in the first two movies.

Yes, some things unfortunately had to be left out of PoA. The complete Marauders backstory, told as a narrative by Lupin in the books, had to be condensed. So we do not see Harry's Patronus as Prongs connect to his father's Animagus, nor is their entire story told. But Harry does come to understand that his father lives on in him. And the remaining Marauders reunite in the Shrieking Shack with the revelations about Peter Pettigrew's identity. Alan Rickman (as Snape) has one of his best scenes ever when he's going after Oldman with the juicy line "Revenge is sweet" and waving a wand in his face. And in turn, Gary Oldman has a ball telling Snape to "Go play with your chemistry set." It's the only movie scene there will ever be with adult Snape vs. Sirius, because David Yates chose to leave out their confrontation in OotP (except sadly as voices through a door). In the end, there is the spectacular werewolf transformation and snarling dog-fight scene. Who could ask for more?

Wait a minute . . . there is more—a lot more—the whole complicated time-turner sequence, which is done with such finesse and good storytelling that even viewers who have not read the books can understand it. An amazing achievement and another great reason this is the best movie.

Harry Potter and the Sorcerer's Stone

Some people may find the first movie bland because it was geared mainly toward children, but in fact, it set the bar originally and none of the others have lived up to it. Nowadays, fans are just jaded and want something different each time, but when *Sorcerer's Stone* first appeared, it seemed the essence of magic. Actually, it still is. It set the standards for all the other films in the series, so director Chris Columbus should be praised for what he created. Everything had to be built from scratch, and Hogwarts-type locations in Oxford and Scotland had to be discovered for the first time. Everything from the school uniforms, to the Common Rooms, to the food in the Great Hall had to appear true to the books. And they had to take pains to get the script just right with the help of J.K.R., because if this movie had been too lame or cheesy, there might not have been a second or third. Instead, it is still a delight to watch, with Daniel Radcliffe, Rupert Grint, Emma Watson, and Tom Felton all adorably young at the beginning of their careers. The casting of all the actors is impeccable, and this movie has the best Dumbledore of all: the late Richard Harris, who captured the humor, whimsy, and dignity of the headmaster better than Michael Gambon has so far.

Most of the scenes in *Sorcerer's Stone* are classics, from Harry waking up in his Cupboard Under the Stairs, to the multitude of owls on the rooftops (how did they do that?) to the letters flying down the chimney. Nothing is more satisfying than watching Hagrid, played by the great Robbie Coltrane, blow the door off the Dursleys' hiding place and announce, "You're a wizard, Harry!" Then we get our first glimpse of Diagon Alley and the magical shops that have a Victorian look about them. Columbus did a great job conveying Harry's sense of wonder and "inventing" this world for the first time, especially the thrilling Quidditch matches on a field decorated as if for a Renaissance tournament.

And maybe this movie is not just for kids. Don't forget the screaming book in the dark library, the scary creature drinking blood from the dead unicorn, and Harry's sadness when viewing his parents in the Mirror of Erised. Those scenes are just as powerful to adults as they are to children. The ending has true suspense as the children navigate the obstacle course of Fluffy the three-headed dog, the Devil's Snare, and the living chess set. The revelation of the Professor Quirrell-Voldemort combo at the end is bizarre and shocking, and it's exciting when the kids win the house cup. Yes, of course, it all happens in the book too, but it wouldn't be the best movie if we didn't recognize Harry's world and want to revisit it again and again.

Verdict

Sorcerer's Stone *set the stage and the "look" of the whole series, but* Prisoner of Azkaban *added an aura of mystery and darkness. The first movie had a ready-made audience of children, but* Prisoner of Azkaban *had to keep the interest of teenagers and adults alike. Considering the amazing number of special effects and new characters, plus an extra-complicated time-turning plot, the verdict is that* Prisoner of Azkaban *sets the standard for what a top-notch HP movie should be.*

Is it appropriate for Harry to use Unforgivable Curses?

Yes!

It is appropriate for Harry to use Unforgivable Curses because he has very justifiable reasons each time. After Sirius is pushed through the Death Veil in OotP, Harry has to go after Bellatrix and try to stop her. It's only logical. And to slow her down, he tries to do the Cruciatus Curse on her. Yes, it's true that he is taught in GoF never to use an Unforgivable because the Ministry considers them illegal, but come on—the kid has just seen his godfather murdered! Of course he would lash out to avenge Sirius, and Bellatrix is a horrible Death Eater who has escaped from Azkaban, so she deserves it. And there is a sense of justice since *Crucio* is the spell she used to torture Neville Longbottom's parents into insanity, as Harry learns in GoF. But Harry fails at doing the Cruciatus on Bellatrix anyway, because he doesn't really intend to—even if he thinks he did.

In HBP, Harry tries to do the Cruciatus Curse on Snape as he flees from the tower. Again, Harry has just witnessed a murder and is out of his mind with rage. He wants to stop the man he blames for Dumbledore's death. But Snape is able to deflect the Cruciatus Curse both times, and shouts: "No Unforgivable Curses from you, Potter!" [HBP, p. 602]. Snape is just lucky because Harry really means to hurt him. The boy can't have known that Dumbledore's death was planned in advance, and that Snape never wanted to do it, which he discovers in DH. But Harry does what is appropriate given what he knows at the time—any Auror would do the same to an escaping criminal. Even if he'll be sorry later, it all makes sense at the time.

The last time Harry uses *Crucio* is in DH, and it's probably the time that is most questionable. When Amycus Carrow spits in the face of Minerva McGonagall, Harry doesn't hesitate to give him the full force of the Cruciatus Curse. This time the spell works perfectly. Harry admits later that he enjoyed it because this time he really meant it. He gives credit to Bellatrix for teaching him this [DH, p. 593]. But hey—all is fair in war, and the Battle of Hogwarts had just started. Carrow was a Death Eater, and Harry knew that both Carrow and his twisted sister had been torturing members of Dumbledore's Army and younger children, so there was no reason to spare them pain. Harry isn't right to react in this way—but it is at least somewhat forgivable, and while McGonagall tells Harry it was foolish, she also says he was being gallant to defend her. So the bottom line is that it doesn't bother McGonagall all that much, and Harry certainly never goes to jail for it, so the *Crucio* is appropriate for the circumstances. Harry knows that in times of war the rules are different, and it is important to meet fire with fire.

Pain is a side effect of war. Harry had to know how to use the same spells the Death Eaters were going to use on him, or he might have died. After all, when Molly Weasley duels Bellatrix in DH, she must use an Unforgivable Curse to kill her. She's a good character, too, but isn't that appropriate during a battle? Harry shouldn't be held to a higher moral standard than anyone else when he is fighting for his life.

No!

They're not called the Sometimes-Forgiveable Curses—they're called the Unforgiveable Curses, and for good reason. Even the Muggle nations (mostly) agree—torture is *never* the answer, and there is *never* an appropriate time for Harry to cast an illegal Unforgivable Curse. Battle or no battle, it is wrong. And Harry never shows any remorse or questions his own judgment about that, which sends a really bad message to young readers. If Harry is a true hero, why does he resort to torture as revenge? Yes, he feels human feelings of rage and grief because people have died. But torturing someone is the lowest thing one human being can do to another, and it's sadistic—Harry has to enjoy it in order to cast the spell. Also, having been the victim of the Cruciatus Curse himself (when Voldemort attacked him in the graveyard), Harry knows *exactly* how painful it is and what he is doing to his own victims. It is just unbelievable that he could keep trying the Cruciatus Curse until he got it right, and then enjoy it. That's not the Harry the fans thought they knew! It shows a complete lack of control over his emotions.

In every battle scene, Harry proves that he knows other spells that can stop people in their tracks. In the Battle of the Tower in HBP, the best spells are *Impedimenta*, which makes people fall over, and *Petrificus Totalus*, or the Body-Bind Curse, which keeps them from moving at all. Plus, there are other effective charms, jinxes, and hexes, not to mention the Stunning spell *Stupefy* that the kids used at the Department of Mysteries in OotP. So why is it ever necessary for Harry to try an Unforgivable Curse to keep Bellatrix or Snape from running away? Since when is painful revenge a good thing in the books? What about showing mercy? At the end of PoA, Harry stops Sirius and Remus from killing Peter with *Avada Kedavra*, and that is the absolute right thing to do. Everyone in the wizarding world knows the Unforgivables are wrong. Yet every time a situation gets personal for him, Harry tries the *Crucio* because it feels satisfying in the heat of the moment. That makes him no better than Voldemort.

The most depressing and stupid moment is when Harry uses the *Crucio* on Amycus Carrow in Deathly Hallows. We are expected to believe that he uses one of most sinister curses around just because an ugly Death Eater spit at Professor McGonagall? What a stupid reason to inflict ultimate pain on someone! There is absolutely no moral high ground for that, and it's immature and hot-headed. Also, Minerva is dead wrong to thank Harry for it, too. She should have known better than that. It is never right to torture someone over a lady's honor. And what's really crazy about that is in HBP, Harry catches Amycus laughing while trying to *Crucio* Ginny, and stops him from doing it with an *Impedimenta* spell.

So who is worse, Harry or Amycus? It's a sad day when Harry Potter sinks to the level of a Death Eater himself, but that's what happens. Carrow is outnumbered two to one, and Harry or McGonagall could easily turn him into a toad or a centipede and put him in a tin can for life. Harry could use the *Rictusempra* spell he uses on Draco in the second-year dueling club and tickle Carrow to death [CoS, p. 192]. Did Harry forget all the boring forgiveable spells between HBP and DH?

Maybe J.K.R. is trying to show that Voldemort's soul-crux is having an effect on Harry's mind, making his actions similar to the Dark Lord's? Several times in DH Harry sees the world through Voldemort's eyes, such as the death of Severus Snape. Even so, Harry is supposed to have a pure soul, and he can't possibly enjoy torturing people and stay pure. That goes against everything Dumbledore stood for, and it crosses the line between good and evil. Harry should never have used an Unforgiveable Curse on anyone, for any reason.

Verdict

Should Harry be forgiven for his Unforgivable tendencies, since he was seeking justice? Or should the justice system seek him out for breaking laws against the Unforgivables? A life-threatening situation might be understandable, such as a one-on-one duel. But other reasons for using the Cruciatus Curse, *such as anger, sadness, revenge, and especially spitting are probably not defensible in front of the Wizengamot. Verdict: It is never appropriate for Harry to use an Unforgivable Curse.*

Which of these scenes from the books should the filmmakers have left in the movies?

Sometimes with a movie that is based on a book, you can miss what's not there, so these are some things the fans love that were omitted from the movies.

Quidditch (OotP)

The Rupert Grint fans were so looking forward to Ron finally getting his moment of glory on the Quidditch Pitch to the rousing sound of the Slytherin crowd singing the old favorite "Weasley is our King" [OotP, p. 408]. The studios decided not to include Quidditch in this movie even though it is the shortest of the five so far, and it's a shame because it is really Ron's coming-of-age story, with him finding his own way separately from Harry, who is sidelined from Quidditch by Dolores Umbridge. Plus, it would have added some light-hearted moments to a very dark movie, and that could only have been an improvement.

Peeves the Poltergeist

He's not a ghost, but according to J.K.R., he's an entirely different sort of "indestructible spirit of chaos" who looks like a small man [JKR-OS]. Peeves may not be a hugely important character, but it's screwy that the sarcastic sprite was written out of the movies. For one thing, he's wickedly funny, and some of the films need comic relief. A lot of readers were looking forward to seeing Lupin give Peeves a *Waddiwasi* spell in PoA and send gum up his nose. But even more fans wanted Peeves to join in the attack on Umbridge in OotP, with Minerva McGonagall letting him know that the crystal chandelier "unscrews the other way" so he could drop it on Umbridge [OotP, p. 678], and the Weasley twins advising their kindred spirit to "Give her hell from us, Peeves!" [OotP, p. 675]. There is no reason why the caretaker of Hogwarts, Argus Filch, should be in the movies, and not his hysterical arch-nemesis, Peeves.

The film producers might say that Peeves would have been too expensive to create, but that's not true! The movies already have ghosts riding horses, house-elves, Dementors, and paintings with wild animals in them. How much more could it cost to show a little man who floats around throwing chalk at people? Walt Disney was doing that floaty effect back in the 1960s with *Bedknobs and Broomsticks* and *Mary Poppins*. Maybe they thought it would look too much like *Ghostbusters*, but they could have shown him more as a little man in a pointy hat, and not just a Casper-like blobby thing. Peeves is a character everyone loves, and he is in every book, including DH. Since he was never introduced at all in the films, Peeves can't be shown fighting in the Battle of Hogwarts and singing his "Moldy Voldy" victory song [DH, p. 746]. Every movie would have been much more fun with Peeves.

Lily in Snape's Worst Memory (OotP)

No—the worst travesty in all the movies happens in *Order of the Phoenix* when Lily Evans is completely left out of "Snape's Worst Memory." Peeves isn't central to the plot and neither is Quidditch, but Lily Evans Potter is the key to major points, including Snape's anger at Sirius and James, and his willingness to protect Harry. It's insanity that the moviemakers decided to film around that storyline.

We know that the entire memory of Snape being attacked by James and being rescued by Lily was filmed, because those were some of the earliest shots released before OotP came out. Several of the young actors spoke to the press about their roles and dialogue in interviews, including the actress who plays Lily, but there wasn't even an extra scene added to the DVD. And that stinks. It's bad enough that director David Yates concentrated on Umbridge instead of Snape and Occlumency anyway, but to cut "Snape's Worst Memory" to shreds and make it a silent flashing movie without Lily is almost unforgivable.

Here's the thing: Lily has to be in Snape's memory because she is the most important person in his whole life, and Snape's motivation for everything, so what could possibly lead to the decision to leave her scenes on the cutting room floor? That scene is the heart of whole book, and the biggest thing Harry ever learns about his parents [OotP, p. 647]. And not only were the Snape fans upset about it, but the Marauders fans, too. They never got to see James being flirty with his future wife, or see Sirius telling Prongs that Lily thought he was too arrogant. They never saw Lupin afraid to stand up to his only friends, or Peter snickering while watching Snape being tormented. For years, on every discussion forum, fans have debated that scene. It is direct foreshadowing for HBP and DH and it was highly anticipated. Maybe they will cobble it back together somehow for the "Prince's Tale" in the Deathly Hallows movies. Good luck with that, WB. Please put Lily back into Snape's memory where she belongs.

Verdict

Rupert Grint's character has been relegated to a significantly reduced role because of movie edits, and that makes many fans unhappy. Peeves the Poltergeist is also disappointingly missing from the movies. Lily Evans Potter is Harry's mother, but the filmmakers obliviated her from Snape's childhood memory. Which is the worst omission? Verdict: If they meant to concentrate on Harry's own story, then leaving Lily Potter out of OotP is the biggest screwup of the movies.

Who would you like to get to know better: Andromeda Tonks or Blaise Zabini?

Andromeda Black Tonks

It's a shame we only catch a glimpse of Andromeda Tonks in *Deathly Hallows*. Sirius Black calls her his favorite cousin in OotP, but we never hear any stories about their friendship. Being the older sister of Narcissa Malfoy and Bellatrix Lestrange, whom she closely resembles, she is fascinating. We know she was in Slytherin house because Professor Slughorn said in HBP that he knew the whole Black family when he was head of house. So that makes Andromeda a special character: a Slytherin pureblood who marries a Muggle-born. So how did Andromeda escape her pureblood family to run away with Ted Tonks? Were her own parents just like her aunt, crazy Mrs. Black at Grimmauld Place, who burned her name off the family tapestry? It would be interesting to know whether she had any contact with Narcissa after the birth of their children. It's a similar story to that of Lily and Petunia, sisters who live in very different worlds. Andromeda's daughter, Nymphadora, is a Metamorphmagus, or shape-shifter, and she tells Harry in OotP that the trait is genetic. So did she inherit it from Andromeda? Did Sirius like her so much because she could transfigure so easily?

It's interesting that Harry raises his voice at Andromeda in DH, and based on her appearance alone judges her to be arrogant just like Bellatrix or Narcissa. When will Harry learn not to judge a book by its cover, or a Slytherin by a proud demeanor? Andromeda is distressed at that moment because she thinks her only daughter might be dead, which sadly comes true by the end of the book. After the fall of Voldemort, and after the death of Ted Tonks, Andromeda alone raises Harry's godson, Teddy Lupin. That's really sad, but also raises more questions. She and Harry must have gotten to know each other quite well over the years, and their conversations must have been rather amazing as they reminisced about the Blacks and Malfoys. Through her memories, he would have learned so much more about Sirius when he was young, a great treat for Harry. It's too bad we didn't see any of this in the books.

Blaise Zabini

What an interesting character Blaise Zabini is, yet we hardly see him in the books. His name is called out last in the alphabetical order system for the Sorting Hat in SS, but there is nothing about him until HBP, when he shows up sitting with the other Slytherins on the train to Hogwarts. It was a surprise to some fans that he was a young man, since his gender was unknown and many thought that Blaise could just as well be a feminine name. But indeed, he turns out to be a handsome boy with a proud manner. For some reason he suddenly appears with Draco Malfoy and his gang though they never had anything to do with him in the other books. Pansy Parkinson teases him in HBP about liking Ginny Weasley, and he says he couldn't care less about a blood traitor, but Harry is immediately jealous of him all the same.

At the meeting of the Slug Club, Professor Slughorn asks Blaise all about his mother, a beautiful woman with the nasty habit of marrying rich men who tended to die suddenly after their weddings, leaving her a wealthy woman. That sounds like a great story, but we only have that one tantalizing detail. What sort of life did Blaise have growing up with a succession of new fathers? Did he ever know his own father? And what about his rather disturbing mother with her possibly murderous lifestyle? Blaise shows curiosity when Draco mentions becoming a Death Eater in HBP, so we know he has not yet taken that drastic step, and it is unclear if he ever will. Is he really that much like Draco? What happens to him during the Battle of Hogwarts? Does he marry someone in Harry's circle of acquaintances? Does Harry ever get to know him?

Verdict

Andromeda Tonks is the unknown Black sister, and Blaise Zabini is the mysterious Slytherin. In spite of a family resemblance to Bellatrix, Andromeda is good at heart, which is proven by her marriage and her delightful daughter, Nymphadora Tonks. But what is Blaise really like? Should we believe that he is just another throwaway Slytherin destined for bad things? Verdict: Tell us more, lots more, about Blaise Zabini.

Are the HP books for adults or children?

For Adults

There is nothing childish about the Harry Potter books as is evidenced by the millions of adult fans seen reading them on subways and airplanes. These books have no age barriers with their intricate plotlines and flawed characters. It's true that Harry is an innocent child at the beginning, but his life is already marred by the death of his parents and the abuse from the Dursley family. So the series isn't a comforting story of wish fulfillment for kids, but a tale of near-tragedy written on an adult level. Yes, the fantastic magic and the lighthearted humor are there for all ages. But most adults come back to the books for the complicated adult characters such as Albus Dumbledore, Severus Snape, Sirius Black, Remus Lupin, and Bellatrix Lestrange. Adults can read between the lines and see nuances of character that children never see.

J.K.R. doesn't try to tone it all down, because she is writing for herself and never pulls any punches: People curse each other in anger, raise their voices, fight and bleed, feel lust and unrequited love, contemplate suicide, abuse alcohol and potions, and even become deadbeat parents. The Death Eaters, Lord Voldemort, and werewolves like Fenrir Greyback are similar to real-life sociopaths, preying on children, mentally and physically abusing people, and committing murder. And the good folks don't always walk the straight and narrow either, but have to choose between what is right and what is easy. Even Harry faces moral dilemmas and sometimes takes a turn to the Dark Side. And all the characters change and grow in every book, some showing painful remorse, and others dying unrepentant. J.K.R. could have kept it all shallow and fun for the kiddies, but she wove in the darkness and depth to create a place where adults could feel the danger. The children do not remain pure and simple, but grow into complex passionate adults.

So an adult reader may start out viewing the books as a variation of C. S. Lewis's Narnia, but will discover a plot out of Greek tragedy. These books are more like Stephen King's *The Shining*, than R. L. Stine's *Goosebumps* for kids. Think *Macbeth* instead of *The Wizard of Oz*. The true philosophical depth would go right over the head of the average child, with long passages about the state of Voldemort's soul, Dumbledore's view of good and evil, and Hermione's philosophical musings about death. Then there are the family trees of the Blacks, Gaunts, and Peverells, like a wizarding version of the royal history of Great Britain. It's the adult readers who love to sift through the tidbits of mythology, alchemy, and the hero's journey. It's rare in the world for a series to keep an adult audience hooked for so many years. But in this case, it's the grown-ups who have been buying the books all along.

For Children

The Harry Potter books are obviously not written for adults: The publishers list them as children's books, and so do most bestseller lists. Everything in the story is seen through the eyes of a young and not-altogether-quick-witted boy who, like all children, needs a fair bit of help interpreting his world. Adults may smile at Harry's confusion, but they can't really identify with him. He is fearless but not the brightest light, and has to be led around by geniuses like Hermione the Bookworm or Dumbledore the Wise. Sometimes, Harry is rescued by his sidekicks: Ron Weasley the Honest and True and Neville Longbottom, the Boy-Who-Overcomes-Fear. The plot is just a simple action-adventure, with flying horses and cars, dragon battles, and wizard duels. Who else but a child would appreciate such predictable fairy tales?

Everything is simplified in black and white, with Harry separating the world into people he likes or doesn't like, with predictable bad guys and inspirational good guys. The characters in between are mostly forgettable, but there are also the strong stereotypes of the "mean teacher" or the "nice mommy who cooks a lot." If this were an adult book, then instead of Harry becoming a child hero, which rarely happens in adult books, Voldemort, with his political control of the government, would probably be the winner. The triumph of darkness would be explored in depth and detail. As it is, the government is bumbling and Harry is smarter than both prime ministers. Voldemort is just a weak baddie for Harry the child to destroy. The Dark Lord could never truly win because that would not be appropriate for children, and that's why there has to be a happily-ever-after Epilogue for Harry and Ginny in their safe, sunny, and segregated Gryffindor-centric world.

Granted J.K.R. is a writer who loves details, and children and adults can appreciate the fantastic beasts and magical spells. But the author also relies on embarrassing sight gags such as Ron being attacked by an aquarium full of B-movie brains, Snape being turned into a bag lady, or Hagrid singing a lullaby to his baby dragon. Cousin Dudley is fat, so of course, he gets a pig's tail, and Neville is meek, so of course, he wears bunny slippers. It's predictable and certainly not written for adults. However, kids love it when something feels "right" to them in the books, and J.K.R. gives them what they crave. The Marauders take risks and look handsome, so of course, they are the coolest of the cool kids. The pretty girls like Lily, Ginny, and Cho have the best magical skills, which makes them worthy of heroes such as James, Harry, and Cedric. The worst villains have no sense of humor but are, nevertheless, unintentionally funny. Dolores Umbridge is carried away by centaurs, and later uses Mad-Eye Moody's eyeball as a surveillance camera. Death Eaters are turned into "baby heads" at the Department of Mysteries. Peter Pettigrew squeaks more than a murderer should when he has to feed baby Voldemort his bottle of venom at bedtime. Bellatrix Lestrange is just the cackling wicked witch from *Hansel and Gretel*.

There is nothing wrong with a simple hero tale for children, and Harry Potter is one of the best ones ever written. But there's a reason these books are listed as children's book: Even if Jo didn't intend to do so, she wrote the series primarily for the appreciation of children—and adults with good imaginations.

Verdict

This debate will never go away. Are the books dark adult novels with complex characters? Or are they simple childhood fantasies filled with stereotypes? Are the adult fans just victims of arrested development, or are the children who read them precocious beyond their years? Verdict: This one is a draw—Jo struck a happy balance. The books are written for adults, children, and any human on the planet who can read.

If you could go back in time and talk J.K. Rowling into changing something in the books, what would you change?

Show the Courtship of Lily and James

If Lily thought that James was an "arrogant bullying toe-rag" for most of her time at Hogwarts, then what made her change her mind [OotP, p. 647]? How did James charm her and win her love? Was it just good looks and money, plus the fact that they were both cool kids in Gryffindor? We know they got married and had baby Harry, but beyond that their relationship is rather mysterious. A few added scenes from a diary or some love letters could easily fix that. How did James prove he was no longer a bully? Did he really change or did he lie to her? Where did they go on that first date? Did Sirius think it would work out? Surely there was no love potion involved—or maybe there was? Enquiring minds want to know.

Let Harry and Snape Work Out Their Problems

The Snape fans of the world hoped beyond hope that he and Harry would have a big emotional confrontation to work out their problems. Fans thought J.K.R. was hinting at this when she made the statement after HBP that: "Harry-Snape is now as personal, if not more so, than Harry-Voldemort" [JKR-MN]. Harry and Snape were like fire and gasoline, and readers wanted to see that interaction again, but maybe with more honesty on both sides. Snape might have learned he could trust Harry, and, in return, Harry could have grown up and seen why Dumbledore's trust wasn't misplaced in Snape.

It would have been difficult for Snape to blurt out that he always loved Lily Potter, and that's probably why J.K.R. chose to do it in a memory in DH instead. But if Snape and Harry had talked it out, they still could have used the Pensieve for the memories to make it easier for Harry to believe the truth. And after Harry got over the shock, he might finally have accepted that Snape had a heart.

It would just be so satisfying and brutally honest, and it would be much better than Snape's death scene, when Harry is numb and emotionless, and basically sees the death through the cruel eyes of Voldemort. The mind connection with Voldemort might have ruled out a heart-to-heart talk, but this is a magical story and Voldie was distracted for most of DH. Anything could have been possible if J.K.R. had wanted to write it that way. If only Harry had used a Shield Charm on Snape just before the snake got him in the throat, they might have worked out their bad karma and admitted to each other for once that they are on the same side. It would have been a good lesson for the younger readers, too, if both Harry and Snape could have admitted their mistakes and learned to work together in spite of their differences. That sort of resolution is missing throughout the books, and here was a chance for real unification of the houses of Hogwarts, with Snape as a Slytherin and Harry a Gryffindor. They were always on the same side, but it would have been great to hear them admit it and hug it out. Or, um, at least talk.

Verdict

What do the fans want J.K.R. to add to the books? A big shout-fest of truth between Snape and Harry? Or a scene of sweet young love between Hogwarts hotties James Potter and Lily Evans? Watching a Harry/Snape cuddle session would be fun, but we're suckers for learning about the Potters' past. Verdict: What exactly did Lily see in James? Jo, we must know!

Should Harry Potter be included with the classics of literature?

No

Only time will tell which books are "classics," and the Harry Potter books have not been around long enough to earn a place on that list. Sure, they have been popular with modern readers for quite a few years, but the series is over now and recently, the books have been knocked from the bestseller list. With no new material from the Potterverse on the horizon, and other books for young readers coming along all the time, it's possible that Harry Potter may eventually fade from the literary scene except in children's libraries.

And, perhaps that is as it should be, since the Potter books are a hodge-podge of elements from every fairy tale and children's classic ever written. Even with original and memorable characters, the plotlines are derivative of everything from Homer's *The Iliad* and Greek mythology, to horror stories and the Hardy Boys mysteries. Harry is an orphan, which is a cliché of children's stories. That proves that there are no new plots in the world, but tugging at the heartstrings is a great way to sell books. It doesn't, however, make a book a classic. Neither does comparing it to great achievements in fantasy, such as Tolkien's works. Obviously, J.K.R. modeled Dumbledore after Gandalf, right down to his long white beard and brilliant mind. But J. R. R. Tolkien created an entirely new world, with maps and mythology surrounding the men, elves, dwarves, and hobbits who speak completely original languages invented by Tolkien. Rowling, on the other hand, uses nothing but the English language and a sprinkle of Latin, some British genealogy, and an ordinary landscape with suburban homes and alleyways near the main streets of London. So the Potter books do not compare.

Most students discover classic books in reading groups at school, but honestly, it is difficult to see how Harry Potter could be taught in the classroom. The storylines are just too complicated, and none of the books stand alone. What teacher has the time to explain relationships between fifty characters per book, or the meanings of twenty spell-words? And what purpose would it serve besides reading for fun and pleasure? The Harry Potter series, brilliant as it is, simply has not contributed much to literary convention. It's not unique and does not deserve to be treated as anything other than a good take on old ideas.

Yes

Of course the Harry Potter books deserve to be included with literary classics. The reason books become classics in the first place is because they are popular, and no series has ever come close to matching the popularity of the Harry Potter series. Over 400 million copies have been sold to date. Some scholars may think that because a book is written for a general audience, it can't have classic status. But let's remember that Shakespeare's plays were written for royalty and commoners alike and had a lot of comedy and tragedy mixed together, just like Harry Potter.

One reason for that popularity is that Harry Potter is a coming-of-age story in the tradition of Mark Twain's *The Adventures of Tom Sawyer* and L. M. Montgomery's *Anne of Green Gables*. And yes, like those famous characters, Harry is an orphan, and the orphan tale is a classic element of literature. The main character suffers grief and loss at an early age, but succeeds against the odds due to special gifts. It's a theme everyone in the world can understand because all children feel misunderstood or mistreated, and the characters generate sympathy. Harry also goes on a journey of discovery, feeling very alone, much like the motherless *Huckleberry Finn* or the children of widower Atticus Finch in Harper Lee's *To Kill a Mockingbird;* those children learn to look beyond the prejudices of their time and see the humanity around them. Harry and others do learn those lessons with Hagrid, the house-elves, and even the Slytherins. So the message is every bit as powerful as the ones in some of the greats of the literary world.

But Harry isn't the only character who reminds us of classic literature. The story of Tom Riddle, a boy raised in an institution when his mother dies giving birth, is right out of *David Copperfield* by Charles Dickens. As Tom grows up, he follows the philosophy of Machiavelli's *The Prince*, seeking power ruthlessly in a desire to take over the world. He becomes a monster, rather like Robert Louis Stevenson's *Dr. Jekyll and Mr. Hyde*, or Mary

Shelley's *Frankenstein*. And the way Dumbledore and Harry track down the secrets of Tom Riddle's evil deeds is worthy of the great Sherlock Holmes stories by Arthur Conan Doyle.

Then there is Severus Snape, the dark antihero of the tale, who resembles the tormented Heathcliff in Emily Bronte's *Wuthering Heights*. Heathcliff is an "abandoned boy," like Snape, and his childhood friend, Cathy, becomes the love of his life; her later rejection drives him to despair. For Snape, it is the death of Lily Evans Potter that causes his grief, but, unlike Heathcliff, he tries to overcome his dark side. As the young Half-Blood Prince, Snape is an innocent child in his oversized hand-me-down coats looking much like *The Little Prince* of Antoine de Saint-Exupery, who worries about his "Flower," which parallels Snape and his concern for Lily. Both The Little Prince and Severus Snape are killed by a snake, which echoes another character, the legendary hero *Beowulf*. That character is attacked in a dark lair by a serpent, and as Beowulf dies he wants only to see his "treasure" once more: For Snape, that means the green eyes of Lily Potter. There are even traces in Snape of *The Count of Monte Cristo* by Alexandre Dumas, about a man who is torn from his true love, but seeks perfect revenge on those who destroyed his happiness.

J.K.R. has mentioned before that one of her models as a writer is Jane Austen's *Emma*, and that is perhaps why romance in Harry's world is similarly fraught with misunderstandings, lost loves, confusion, and jealousy. People are not what they seem at first glance, and love can be surprising, as Harry learns himself with Cho and Ginny, and later with the relationship of Remus Lupin and Nymphadora Tonks. The pureblood wizarding families arrange marriages to protect the bloodline, but those are not always the happiest of unions, which is a mirror of British society in Austen's *Pride and Prejudice*. In that book, the characters instinctively know that the best love is spontaneous and freely given, a major theme of all the Harry Potter books.

As high fantasies, the Potter books are right up there with Tolkien's *Lord of the Rings* and C. S. Lewis's *Narnia* series. But those aren't the only similar classics. J. K. Rowling has said many times she based some of the fantasy elements on *The Little White Horse* by Elizabeth Goudge, as well as E. Nesbit's *The Book of Dragons* and *The Phoenix and the Carpet*. When Harry is whisked away from the everyday Muggle world to another dangerous place where there are good and bad witches, he follows the same yellow brick road as

Dorothy (still another orphan) in L. Frank Baum's *The Wizard of Oz*. And, of course, Harry is almost literally *Through the Looking Glass*, where everything is backwards from the real world, just as in Lewis Carrol's *Alice in Wonderland*. Hagrid's love of animals is much like the generous *Dr. Dolittle* created by Hugh Lofting; the Weasleys in the Burrow manage to survive like the tiny Clock family in Mary Norton's *The Borrowers*; and, of course, everyone flies around doing magic like *Peter Pan* by J. M. Barrie and *Mary Poppins* by P. L. Travers. The list is probably endless, but the Harry Potter books have a permanent place among these great works of art.

Verdict

Does a book have to be around for fifty or even one hundred years in order to be a classic? Or, is there such a thing as an instant classic that people can appreciate on many levels right away? A true classic probably has both the continuing audience and the recognizable motifs that stand the test of the ages. Since the Harry Potter books meet both standards, the verdict is: Yes, the Harry Potter books belong on bookshelves alongside the all-time great novels.

Is Xenophilius Lovegood a traitor?

Yes!

No matter how funny or charming he is, Mr. Lovegood is one of the biggest traitors in the whole series. In DH, he tries to sell Harry, Hermione, and Ron to the Death Eaters! He should have realized that there was a better way to save Luna from the Death Eaters and that Harry would have helped him track her down, but that doesn't seem to enter his mind. And even if his daughter was in mortal peril at the time, that's no excuse. The Weasleys had kids who were in the same danger for years because Harry was their friend, but Mr. and Mrs. Weasley would never betray Harry to save one of their own children.

So Mr. Lovegood is just a big coward. As editor of *The Quibbler* magazine, he absolutely knows how evil Voldemort is. It's pathetic that a journalist who believes in freedom of expression would fall apart in the middle of the war. Putting Harry on the cover of the magazine as "Undesirable Number One" was just propaganda for the Dark Side [DH, p. 419]. And what a fool he is to trust the Death Eaters anyway—killers don't keep promises, so ultimately, he is being naïve and weak. Even though he is Obliviated by Hermione so he'll forget what he's done, he still should be court-martialed and convicted of war crimes, or at least charged with conspiring with the enemy.

No!

Mr. Lovegood's only crime is loving his daughter too much. Who can blame a father for wanting to ensure the safety of his beautiful daughter Luna? Isn't that what parents are for? He is a widower and Luna is his only child, and that's a totally different situation from the Weasleys. Also, Mrs. Weasley has watched Harry and Hermione grow up and loves them like family— she has a very different relationship with them than Xenophilius does. Mr. Lovegood has criticized Voldemort in *The Quibbler*, so he surely feels guilty for making Luna a target. Her empty bedroom covered in cobwebs must be a constant reminder of his failure to protect her, and he sadly suffers as much as anyone in the book. Since he was already sort of mentally whacked-out to begin with, losing his daughter may have been the little push he needed to tip over the edge.

And since he believes that Harry was The Chosen One, Mr. Lovegood probably figures that Harry is going to survive no matter what happens. So looking at it from his point of view, why should his Luna have to be sacrificed and held for ransom when Harry's magical protection is so much stronger? That may be selfish on his part, but surely Harry understands what a tough situation it is. When Mr. Lovegood blocks the door so the Trio can't leave his house, he reminds Harry of Lily's courage when she protected him as a baby. And without Lovegood's help, Harry could never have figured out the Deathly Hallows and the Elder Wand, so something good came out of their encounter after all. Hermione is certainly ready to forgive the man right away, even if Ron is not. Since Harry helps Luna escape from Malfoy Manor later in DH, it all turns out for the best. No harm, no foul.

Verdict

Is Mr. Lovegood the lowest kind of traitor, or is he just a father haunted by a Wrackspurt of despair? Should he be dragged off to Azkaban, or should he stay in his eccentric home with his printing press and dirigible plums? Let's recall that Mr. Lovegood is being blackmailed, just as Draco has been over the safety of his parents, and he is acting out of love. We can guess that Dumbledore would have shown him mercy, just as Hermione does. Verdict: Mr. Lovegood is never a real traitor (and he won't remember what he's done anyway due to Obliviation).

Whose death is the saddest?

Sirius Black

No character seems more energetic and alive than Harry's godfather, Sirius Black, so it's incredible that he dies so suddenly. He is so brave, he makes all the other Gryffindors look like little Peter Pettigrews in comparison. After an exciting youth spent running around with the Marauders and rebelling against Lord Voldemort, Sirius is framed for the deaths of the Potter family, as well as twelve Muggles when Peter Pettigrew blows up a street and escapes. Sirius is sent to Azkaban prison, where he wastes away and blames himself for everything, only coping with the Dementors by assuming his Animagus form as a big, shaggy black dog.

But things start looking up for him after he escapes and enters Harry's life. He is Harry's friend and father figure, as well as his faithful dog Snuffles when running around in Animagus form. For Sirius, being with Harry is almost like being back with James, and they both believe that Sirius will be cleared of his crimes by the Ministry, once they realize he is not guilty. The time Harry and Sirius spend at Grimmauld Place, though brief, is a joy for both of them, and for many readers those chapters in OotP are some of the best in the whole series.

Yet once again, Voldemort has to ruin Harry's happiness by targeting someone close to him. Thanks to the house-elf Kreacher's treachery, that person was unfortunately Sirius Black. In OotP, Harry is tricked into thinking that Sirius is being tortured, so he gathers his friends to go and rescue Sirius only to find out it is a trap to lure them to the Ministry. And then the tables are turned and Sirius arrives to help save Harry, and it almost works out with a happy ending—Dumbledore arrives and the fighting almost stops. But Sirius taunts his cousin Bellatrix during their duel, underestimating her willingness to destroy anyone opposed to the Dark Lord. And then she strikes, her spell pushing Sirius backward through the Veil of Death where he disappears with a look of surprise on his face. And millions of readers gasped in horror.

Sirius is such a cool character that readers could scarcely believe J.K.R. would kill him off—what a waste! But he probably needed to be out of the way so that Harry could face his destiny alone in HBP and DH. However, there is no doubt that the Potterverse was a lot darker and more menacing without his cheery arrogance and bark-like laugh. He has so much potential and then suddenly he is just snuffed out in the prime of his life. There were many theories that he would return to Harry's side by the end of the series, either back through the veil or through the two-way mirror he gave Harry as a parting gift. But no, Sirius can't return from the dead, and he doesn't even have a grave like Dobby or Dumbledore. But in DH, when Harry uses the Resurrection Stone, Sirius appears in a younger and more handsome form, to guide him through the forest. For Harry and many fans, Sirius will never truly be gone.

Albus Dumbledore

Since Dumbledore is friends with Nicholas Flamel, one of the oldest men alive at 665 years old as we learn in SS, he surely would have learned some tricks for living a long life. So readers can't accept that Dumbledore's health is going downhill in HBP, even with the hints about Snape having to save him after Dumbledore put on the cursed Peverell ring that blackened his hand. Toward the end of the book, he is still able to roar back with a huge ring of magical fire when some undead Inferi attacks in Voldemort's cave, so in HBP it seemed only logical to think that Dumbledore still had a lot of life left in him.

But Snape merely gives Dumbledore a reprieve from death—a type of life support that can't last. He would have died naturally after a year when the curse grew stronger, but on top of that Dumbledore also drinks an evil potion in the Inferi cave. And on top of that, he makes Snape promise to kill him so the Death Eaters such as Fenrir Greyback won't mutilate his body [DH, p. 683]. Secretly, Dumbledore has other plans about his death, such as wanting Snape to be master of the Elder Wand and to bury it in Dumbledore's tomb so it won't ever be used again. That doesn't work out for Snape, but Harry does become master of the wand, and that saves his own life.

It's heartbreaking that Snape has to agree to carry out such a plan for the one man in the world who trusts him. Dumbledore is like the good father Snape never had, and Harry thinks of him as a wise old grandfather. They both have to watch him die and fall off the tower in one of the most emotionally devastating scenes of the entire series. Dumbledore sees death as just another natural step, and faces it bravely, but fans hoped beyond hope that he would still be alive and that Snape just faked the *Avada Kedavra* somehow. Alas, he was really dead, broken at the bottom of the tower. But in DH he appears to Harry in a peaceful vision of heaven, just as calm and wise as ever, giving advice and apologizing for his own weaknesses in life. And his portrait will always remain in the headmaster's office, waiting to talk to Harry's children when they have problems at Hogwarts and need a kind word or someone who is a good listener.

Dobby the House-Elf

No matter how many deaths there are in DH, it is huge shock when Dobby the house-elf dies in the saddest way possible, stabbed through the heart. As his final act, Dobby stares at Harry, his tiny hands raised as if pleading for help and the last words he says are "Harry Potter," as if they are best friends or brothers. Why does Harry have to lose such a sweet and loyal friend?

Dobby dies after returning bravely to Malfoy Manor, where the family had once made the elf punish himself daily. And once again, his own family betrays him, with Bellatrix calling him a "dirty little monkey" just before giving him the fatal blow [DH, p. 474]. It's such a lowly and disrespectful way for Dobby to die, killed by someone who thinks that house-elves have no feelings. Like the death of Sirius Black, it happens almost as an afterthought, as Dobby is leaving. Like the death of Cedric Diggory, it serves no purpose, except to cause misery.

Dobby is the most childlike character in the books. Unlike many of the wizards who die, Dobby is not big and strong or warlike in any way. A gentle soul, he should have been at Hogwarts baking cakes, with a tea cozy on his head and mismatched socks on his feet. His death is Harry's loss of innocence.

No other character except Dumbledore has a funeral, and Dobby's is actually much more moving. In DH, Harry digs the grave alone, without magic, and he slowly realizes that grief is keeping the power of Dark Lord away from his mind [DH, p. 478]. The other children gather for the funeral: Ron gives Dobby a pair of socks; Luna gently closes his green eyes for the last time and he seems to be sleeping. They each stand around the grave thanking Dobby for his rescue, as if his spirit can hear them (Luna believes that he can). Then Harry is alone again, stacking stones where Dobby will sleep for eternity, and making the proper epitaph: "Here Lies Dobby, A Free

Elf" [DH, p. 481]. He was free to live, but also free to die for Harry. Rest in Peace, Dobby.

Severus Snape

There is one major character who dies misunderstood and in painful anguish: Potions Master Severus Snape. He has one of the most horrific deaths in the entire series—in DH, he is overpowered by the giant snake, Nagini, seized by the neck. Subsequently, he bleeds to death before Harry's eyes. No doubt, some readers cheered as he fell, thinking he deserved it. Even Harry coldly feels nothing except hatred because to him, Snape is a Death Eater, a murderer of Dumbledore, and his worst teacher of all time. But that's an illusion. Snape teaches Harry something important, even in death, through the memories of his sad, lonely life. And later Harry realizes that Snape was trapped, not just by the snake, but by the schemes and intrigues of both Dumbledore and Voldemort. Snape was always trapped and never really had a chance to live—what a waste!

Like Dobby, Snape dies looking into Harry's eyes. But it's a lot more meaningful that Snape wants to do that because he never worshiped Harry, and the boy certainly had no warm, fuzzy feelings for Snape in return. The death doesn't make Harry weep or dig a grave, but that's exactly why it's so sad—Snape was bitter, yes, but a good guy at heart, yet when he dies, no one cares. Voldemort just wants to get rid of him so he can take Snape's wand, and leaves him there in the Shrieking Shack, a place Snape had hated since childhood. Dumbledore never means for Snape to die, as he tells Harry in "King's Cross," calling Snape "Poor Severus" because he is left in the dark about the Elder Wand too long, which leads to a death that is tragic. Snape could have defeated Voldemort if he had been master of the Elder Wand, but instead he became another victim.

It's a shame that Harry and Hermione don't try to save Snape's life, because he had always tried to save them in the past. Snape's last words are "Look at me" as his eyes meet Harry's for one last time [DH, p. 658]. But why? Harry only finds out later from Snape's memories that he had deep feelings for Harry's mother, Lily, who also had green eyes, and that she inspired his beautiful silver doe Patronus. It's just heartbreaking that Harry only understands how Snape feels about fifteen minutes *after* Snape dies.

Yet Harry doesn't forget about Snape's sacrifice, and names one of his sons after him. So for Harry, Snape becomes like family through his namesake Albus Severus, and is remembered as the bravest man Harry ever knew [DH, p. 758]. We never see Snape's headstone, nor his headmaster portrait at Hogwarts, but the fact that Harry hasn't forgotten him nineteen years after his death is epitaph enough.

Verdict

Sirius and Dumbledore die untimely deaths before Harry is ready to let them go. Dobby is a childlike and amusing little character who never does any harm, and his death is a wake-up call to Harry. Snape is dark and complicated, but his outward appearance is deceiving and his actions speak louder than words. He is the character who suffers the longest, but his death is more grotesque and chilling than sad. Each death affects Harry in a different way, but each person dies while thinking about Harry's future. Because we see human deaths so often in movies, we have become desensitized to them. But we rarely see animals being killed, so when we do, it's particularly tragic. And Dobby is like Harry's more human-like pet—loyal, loving, and most importantly, completely innocent. Verdict: The other deaths certainly impact Harry more, but Dobby's death twisted open the tear spigots for us the most.

Should Voldemort be pitied or loathed?

Loathed

> "It is our choices, Harry, far more than our abilities,
> that determine who we truly are." —Albus Dumbledore

Voldemort should inspire nothing but loathing, since he has no reason to become as evil as he does. He and Harry have nearly the same type of childhood as orphans, and they both have the same education at Hogwarts. So what excuse is there for Voldemort to turn into the cruelest wizard who ever lived? Was his life really so bad? Most of his teachers were fond of him. He seems to have everything going for him, but he channels his energy into achieving despicable things. That is a choice he makes, and no one forces him into the life of crime. Dumbledore and Slughorn both want to help Tom Riddle, but he never listens to them, and indeed, fools them with the death of Moaning Myrtle, which he blames on Hagrid and Aragog, the giant spider. He even hunts down his own family and murders them in GoF, before going on a rampage of killing to make himself immortal as described in HBP. So he was never the victim, and he doesn't deserve any pity.

Pitied

Young Tom Riddle can't help it that there is insanity in the Gaunt family as we see in HBP, or that his mother decides to die rather than live and take care of him. It's a shame the wizarding world does not insist that magical orphans be raised by magical foster parents, instead of shelving kids like Tom in uncaring Muggle institutions. Many children raised in orphanages never have a mother figure, and so they become detached from other human beings and lack in emotion. That is Tom's problem. He is a victim. His nature is bent before Dumbledore ever comes to get him at the orphanage as we see in the Pensieve in HBP, so anything he learns later at Hogwarts won't change his personality. So everyone should pity him because he is never a complete and healthy human being, even before he tears up his soul to make Horcruxes.

Verdict

Should we loathe Voldemort for his merciless violence and all the pain he causes, or should we pity the man who grew up with no understanding of love? Given that many other characters have childhood problems and learn to cope, such as Lupin, Snape, Luna, Neville, and Harry himself, does Voldemort really have any excuse? A child's environment significantly impacts their route in life, and with such a shabby upbringing, how can we blame him? Verdict: The overarching theme of the series is that love conquers all. There is more to be gained through empathizing with and understanding Voldemort than there is through hating him, so he should be pitied.

Should Harry have chosen a different profession than Auror?

Yes!

There are so many other possible careers for a wizard with Harry's talents besides being an Auror. And think about it—in a time of peace most of his Defense Against the Dark Arts skills will go to waste anyway. Harry shouldn't be a one-note guy, but should branch out and explore his potential.

Harry could do the logical thing and teach Defense Against the Dark Arts at Hogwarts. It's a job that's made for him, and since the one-year curse on the teaching job died with Voldemort, Harry could teach for many years. That would help him stay near his children while teaching a subject he loves, and he would be the most popular teacher ever. Hogwarts is his home more than any place on earth, and he could join Neville Longbottom in the staff room for a cup of coffee every day.

Madam Trelawney has a vision once that Harry will not die early, but will "live to a ripe old age, become Minister of Magic, and have twelve children" [OotP, p. 583]. That sounds like a plan—maybe Harry should consider politics instead of being an Auror. He would be that rare politician who tells the truth and stays honest while in office. By defeating Voldemort and saving the wizarding world not once but twice, he could probably be elected Minister of Magic. He could move mountains for the Ministry and get a lot done.

Speaking of truth and honesty, Harry could mass-produce Felix Felicis and the Polyjuice Potion, (potions that are difficult and time-consuming to brew) and be a wizard entrepreneur like Fred and George. Then he could sell them to wealthy wizards and witches. Then again, ensuring a steady supply of good luck to already lucky people could only serve to increase inequality in the wizarding world. Harry hasn't yet demonstrated any entrepreneurial tendencies, so he would probably need to consume a significant amount of the product he makes!

Or instead of spending the rest of his life chasing bad guys, Harry *could* become a Healer and learn to help people in a different way. After all, Harry spent more time in the hospital wing at Hogwarts than nearly any other student, so surely he would find it fascinating to learn how to put people back together again. Over and over in the books, there are situations in which Harry laments that he doesn't know how to make potions, stop bleeding, cure Dark Curses, or keep people alive. After witnessing so much suffering, he might get a clue that dueling and broom chases aren't the most useful ways to make a living. Harry could find a real cure for Dragon Pox or find new ways to help werewolves. The St. Mungo's Magical Emergency Ward is still an exciting place.

No!

Becoming an Auror is the best career for Harry because his whole life has been about learning to protect himself and others, and by the end of the series he has seen more action than wizarding policemen twice his age. He can't just settle down to a quiet life after that, and needs an outlet for his saving-people thingy. That's basically the job description of an Auror. Harry also realizes in OotP that the wizarding government is corrupt, and that Aurors have just become henchmen for people at the Ministry of Magic, such as Fudge and Umbridge. The Auror named Dawlish isn't so bad, but he seems to just do what he is told with no sense of right and wrong. Harry would rather be like Kingsley Shacklebolt, who risks his job to remain in the Order of the Phoenix, even participating in secret on the Potterwatch radio show in DH (code name Royal). Harry would want to change the system from the inside out, making sure that innocent people aren't being arrested for the wrong reasons, and trying to maintain his own code of right and wrong.

Harry would never go in for politics because he couldn't be that fake, and he's not the kind of social animal that would get elected. Nor would he want to be tied down to Hogwarts after going to school there for so many years, and it wouldn't be the same without Dumbledore or Snape. He could always train recruits for the Auror A-Team with more advanced magic. As for being a Healer, Harry's bedside manner is fine, but he is nothing like Madam Pomfrey. He needs an exciting job that will keep his Defense Against the Dark Arts skills sharp into old age.

Verdict

Has Harry found true happiness as a dark-wizard catcher in the Auror Department? Or does personal fulfillment wait for him in teaching, business, healing, or politics instead? Harry never was much of a student on a good day, and he is always action-oriented, so it's hard to imagine him leading a quiet life even though his evil nemesis Voldemort is dead and gone. Verdict: Harry should keep his day job as an Auror.

What is the worst book?

These two books work as bridges between the other books. The writing is just as enjoyable as the rest of the series, but readers may feel they have lost their way a little as they wander through them. Again, completely subjective analysis to follow!

Order of the Phoenix

Fans read the Harry Potter books for pleasure and enjoyment, so the alienation and teenage tension in OotP is a real downer that makes the book the least enjoyable of the series. The book is slow paced and dull in the beginning, lingering over Harry's angst and anger at the age of fifteen. Even on the day he gets away from the Dursleys, he suddenly lashes out in capital letters at his best friends, completely unfairly. It might stand to reason that he is in a dark place after watching Voldemort's rise from death in GoF, and seeing Cedric Diggory die in cold blood, but that doesn't completely explain why Harry suddenly whines, complains, and moans about every little thing. Maybe he is taking his cue from Sirius Black, who sulks around his gloomy Slytherin house at Grimmauld Place, acting bitter and resentful that Dumbledore won't let him do anything. He and Harry really deserve each other in OotP.

But maybe Sirius has a point about feeling trapped and that his life is monotonous, since the fans get stuck with the same feeling while in that depressing house for nearly the first 200 pages of the book. A lot of that could have been edited out. Housecleaning with Molly might make a nice article for *Witch Weekly*, but it bogs down the story with so-dull-they're-deadly details of spraying doxies and cleaning cupboards. Unlike cooking scenes in the other books, in this book, J.K.R. doesn't even waste time listing the food they eat. Dinner is just an excuse for someone to drone on about what Voldemort might be doing, as if he or she actually knows what Voldemort was doing, which no one does. The Order of the Phoenix seems like a bunch of incompetent people—what exactly are they doing? They're not nearly as cool as their name makes them out to be. They aren't keeping people from dying, and they can barely protect Harry. It's also depressing that Dumbledore has apparently abandoned Harry without telling him why, which only freaks him out later when he starts having visions of snakes and thinks he's turning into a murderous reptile. Too bad he doesn't—at least that would have been exciting!

When Sirius was growing up, he could escape his gloomy homelife by going to Hogwarts, but that doesn't work for Harry in OotP because Dolores Umbridge has taken over the school with her reign of terror. And from the time Harry arrives at school, OotP becomes a sad book about the dangers of educational testing in the wizarding world. No joke—that's probably the worst theme in all the books because it is so mundane: studying for the O.W.L. exams. We are served up one story after another about kids freaking out during testing, and it's a nightmare for Harry, who is also being tortured by Umbridge with her painful black quill. And worst of all, he's being banned from Quidditch!

There are a few bright spots in the gloom of OotP. Harry meets the luminescent Luna Lovegood and helps to form Dumbledore's Army with students from other Hogwarts houses. The Weasley twins also get sweet revenge on Umbridge. (Although, we maintain it would have been funny to see Fred and George following her around the castle making clip-clopping noises!) But the last half of the book goes completely downhill. Snape and Harry clash and attack each other in violent Occlumency lessons, which end abruptly with no explanation, despite their importance. Cho Chang, Harry's love goddess, falls off her pedestal and becomes as weepy and argumentative as he is, so Harry hypocritically breaks up with her. But still, how dare she talk about her problems when his plate is so full? If anyone is going to be sullen and upset, it ought to be Harry.

The ending is quite predictable and formulaic, again with Harry and his pals in danger before a big duel against Voldemort ensues. Again somebody dies, but unbelievably, this time J.K.R. chooses to kill off a major beloved character—Sirius Black. Fans were outraged about his death since he never really had a chance to do anything much for the other 869 pages of the book. Harry goes nuts, trying to *Crucio* Bellatrix, then roaring at Dumbledore, blaming everyone in the world for his problems. He has a tantrum, breaks things, and acts like a complete idiot. The big secret Dumbledore gives Harry to calm him down is the worst anticlimax in the series: Voldemort and Harry may have to fight it out to the death someday, and one of them has to die. Yeah, duh—even Harry might have figured that out on his own. That's not even the complete truth, since Dumbledore conveniently leaves out the whole Horcrux element, not to mention the Deathly Hallows. Too much mystery, not enough real answers.

Chamber of Secrets

OotP may be longer and duller, but for it's short length, CoS has the worst tendency to go down the toilet. Literally. (Well, not actually literally, but you know what we mean). Half of the book takes place in a girl's restroom, and this time the villain is crawling through the pipes of the school. Harry discovers that the Chamber of Secrets is sort of like the septic tank of Hogwarts, down in the bowels of the castle, and then rumors start to swirl that Mudbloods might get tanked by a monster. Harry is flush with the idea that he is a Parselmouth and can speak to snakes, but pressure builds up from other kids who see him as a threat. If all of this seems draining to the reader, it's because it certainly is.

CoS tries to be an action book, but nothing ever really takes off. When Harry and Ron drive the flying Ford Anglia into the Hogwarts grounds, they don't even have a good time, and it just becomes another reason for Snape to rant and rave, threatening to expel the boys from school. The giant spiders that Hagrid finds so adorable get him thrown into Azkaban. Petrified people keep turning up in the hallways, but no one knows why until the Petrified bodies are stacked like cordwood in the hospital wing. Sadly, Dumbledore never gets a clue that he should investigate whether the Chamber is real, but instead spends his time to having hot cocoa with Minerva McGonagall. All the headmaster would have to do is ask his pet phoenix, Fawkes, to show him the way. We know this since the bird is able to find the Chamber at the end of the book and attack the basilisk who lives there. Why Fawkes had never bothered to clean up such a threat to the school in the first place is the real mystery. Wouldn't it have been more loyal to save kids from being Petrified or possessed right off the bat?

There's another major flaw in this book: We know from SS that Harry can talk to snakes because he has a nice conversation with a giant boa at the zoo, and it all seems very polite. If the basilisk in the Chamber of Secrets was so special to Salazar Slytherin, then why doesn't it think to talk to Harry about anything other than killing and eating? It has a brain larger than a boa—why is it so stupid? Even Aragog the spider can talk. The basilisk seems like just a pawn in the game, and while its venom is deadly, it also helps Harry destroy Tom Riddle's diary and keep Voldemort from returning. So it isn't really such a scary monster at all, and it never succeeded in killing a single student. It doesn't even kill Mrs. Norris the cat!

Verdict

In CoS, Harry has to slide down the drainpipe to rescue Ginny, but at least he saves her from Voldemort with some help from Fawkes, the Sorting Hat, and the Sword of Gryffindor. In OotP, Harry puts the "Grim" in Grimmauld Place. His bratty adolescent crisis can't be explained by just the scar on his forehead so maybe J.K.R. should have let him lighten up a bit. Verdict: OotP is the worst book in the series.

Are the Hufflepuffs dismissed as lame?

Yes!

The Hufflepuffs are written off by everyone, including Jo. The Hufflepuff students don't play an important role, and their house is the only one whose Common Room never gets a visit from Harry. While Professor Sprout is competent, and the late Cedric Diggory is an obvious hero, the rest of the Hufflepuffs seem soft and squishy. Even the cute Auror, Nymphadora Tonks, is essentially a weak character who loses her charm in HBP. Hannah Abbot is another one. She is always around somewhere shaking with fear. Not only is she afraid in PoA that Sirius Black has turned into a shrubbery (ooooh—scary!), in OotP she nearly has a nervous breakdown during O.W.L. exams.

In fact, Hufflepuff house seems to be full of victims! Take Justin Finch-Fletchly, who is nearly attacked by a snake in CoS, then later Petrified by the basilisk. He also hides at school because he thinks Harry is the Heir of Slytherin and wants to kill him (which is wrong, of course). Susan Bones is mentioned over and over as Harry's classmate, and she actually talks to Harry in OotP, but only because her claim to fame is that her relatives keep getting zapped by Voldemort. It's too bad that Harry only dates Ravenclaws or Gryffindors, since he could have taken Susan out for a butterbeer and discovered more about her.

The Hufflepuffs are not the cool kids. Ernie McMillan, ever-studious and talkative, has a Patronus that turns out to be a wild boar in DH. Instead of the noble symbol of Hogwarts, the boar represents the fact that he is a boring person, which is sort of true—he sounds like a young politician sometimes. Zacharias Smith is described as irritating, and he grates on Ginny Weasley's nerves so much she hexes him in HBP. But, even worse, he is a coward, who runs over first-year students in his rush to escape during the Battle of Hogwarts in DH. And that's not all—this losing streak runs in the family because Zacharias is a descendent of Helga Hufflepuff herself through his unfortunate relative Hepzibah Smith, a fat old lady who is greedy and vain. She's a symbol of Hufflepuff weakness when she becomes just another victim of Lord Voldemort.

No!

Weak? Dumbledore's Army is full of Hufflepuffs —they fight alongside Harry at the Battle of Hogwarts! It's not weak that Ernie McMillan's Patronus is a boar—that is a huge and dangerous wild animal, and, therefore, his Patronus might be stronger than any of the Gryffindor Trio's. Tonks is a cool and funny Metamorphmagus or shape-shifter, and she gives her life fighting alongside her husband, Professor Lupin, in DH. And remember Cedric Diggory? He is so noble that he was going to give Harry a chance to win the Triwizard Tournament in GoF and deny himself the victory. That he also died at the hand of the most powerful wizard of all time doesn't make him weak—just unlucky, like many characters from every house.

As for Hepzibah Smith, she can't help it that Voldemort wants to kill her and steal the Hufflepuff cup in HBP. Harry's parents were both in Gryffindor—were they weak because Voldemort killed them? Is Hagrid weak because he is described as overweight, or because he is attacked by Death Eaters? Of course not, and Hepzibah Smith is also a lonely old lady, and has more in common with Bathilda Bagshot or Bertha Jorkins—not stupid or weak, but a symbol of the way Voldemort uses people for his own greedy aims. As an equal opportunity killer, he never cares what house someone is in.

These Hufflepuff characters don't come across just as weaklings or cowards. The story is much more complex than that. Hannah Abbot's problems and fears about exams are shared by many other students, including Harry. It's true that Zacharias is not brave, but he is not much more unlikeable than Gryffindor's Seamus Finnigan, who badgers Harry in OotP about his relationship with Voldemort.

Hufflepuffs are hard-working students and loyal friends. They are equal to the other houses in every way. None of them should be dismissed as weak or lame just because they have human flaws, like every other character in the series.

Verdict

Hufflepuffs don't have to be cream puffs, and in many ways they are just as brave as the Gryffindors. So how did they get the reputation as a "lot o' duffers," as Hagrid describes them in SS [p. 80]? While being a coward or victim of evil is not limited to their house, these Hufflepuff characters seem to lack grit, and they could be labeled as the underachievers of the school. The verdict is: Yes, the Hufflepuffs are definitely dismissed as lame.

Are the Gryffindors too glorified?

No!

Harry is the main character so his house is always going to be the most important, and that's why we learn more about Gryffindor than any other house. And obviously J.K.R. wants us to understand the traits of Gryffindor—boldness and courage—since those are what she values most. If Gryffindors sometimes seem full of themselves, it is only because most of them have high self-esteem and a joy for life—that's why they're in Gryffindor. Yet, they are not all brave in the same way—compare the Weasley twins to their brother Percy. Or Dumbledore to Hagrid. Or Hermione to Lavender Brown. Obviously, Percy, Hagrid, and Lavender are never glorified. They are imperfect and sometimes ridiculous characters, and yet they still belong in Gryffindor. For most of the series, Neville Longbottom is a borderline Hufflepuff with a green thumb, and nothing about him is glorified. He has to work hard to learn magic, and struggle to overcome his fears before he finds his inner worth.

It's true that there are a few Gryffindor students who have glory days in the sense of being young, brilliant, and fun-loving. Those are the Marauders and Lily Evans when they are teenagers. James, Sirius, and Remus are often praised by other characters because they were witty, and because they became Harry's heroes. The same could be said for Harry's mom, Lily, who is praised by Slughorn in HBP for her beauty, wit, and skills. But no one would say that Peter Pettigrew, also a Gryffindor, was anything except a traitor and rat supreme as portrayed in PoA. He's the best example of the complexity of Gryffindor because although his own friends see him as weak and cowardly, he actually gets cozy with the dangerous Voldemort and plots to destroy his own friends. He may have sought glory, but he dies in DH by strangling himself with a silver hand that Voldemort gives him as a gift, and that's not too great.

As for the Gryffindors we know best—Hermione, Ron, and Harry—
we get to know all their faults. Hermione is a bossy know-it-all, Ron can
be thoughtless to the point of cruelty, and Harry has a hot temper. That's
hardly the glorification of Gryffindor. Molly and Arthur Weasley are usually
taken for granted by most of society in spite of their courage. Ginny Weasley is a powerful witch, but only Professor Slughorn makes a big deal over
her in HBP, probably just because she resembles Lily Evans. Finally, there is
Dumbledore who is nearly the ideal wizard, yet by the end of the series, we
see his flaws as a one-time racist and hero-worshipper himself. So, he loses
some of his charisma. The more we understand the Gryffindors, the more
real they become, and the less glorious.

Yes!

Who are we kidding here—of course Gryffindor is glorified. In the books,
courage is the answer to every problem, even when characters are rushing
around in a foolhardy way without an escape plan. It's sad when good people
die, but a Gryffindor never bothers to learn anything from past mistakes.
Plunging into danger once again is what they do best, and it never pays to
be cautious because then it wouldn't be a challenge. All that really matters
is to kill or be killed so another Gryffindor can be remembered by a shrine,
tomb, or trophy.

And while the Gryffindors never hesitate to look down on the Slytherins
for being pureblood racists, it's fascinating that the Gryffindors are just as
"clannish." Harry's parents were both Gryffindors, as shown in their Sorting
Hat scene in DH. Harry may like girls from other houses, but those are just
practice dates before HBP, when he comes home to Ginny, a nice argumentative Gryffindor girl. And look at all the Weasleys, with their pureblood
red hair, all in Gryffindor, as are most of their spouses by the end of DH. Is
that the true meaning of house unity—each house glorifies itself, especially
Gryffindor?

The worst part of it is that certain glorious Gryffindors are self-righteous
bullies. James and Sirius are obnoxious bullies in the books, picking on people and breaking rules, as in "Snape's Worst Memory" in OotP. Yet, they are
never punished much by Dumbledore, and James is made head boy so he
can rule the house along with Gryffindor Lily [SS, p. 55]. In fact, the Gryffindors seem to be rewarded instead of punished in every book. The twins are
just as irreverent as the Marauders, using their talents to hex people they

don't like, such as Dudley Dursley with the use of the Ton-Tongue Toffee in GoF. Their little sister Ginny doesn't mind attacking Zacharias Smith for fun with her broom after a Quidditch match in HBP, or doing the Bat-Bogey Hex on him either, which is why Slughorn praises Ginny. It's just as wrong for Slughorn to glorify Gryffindor as it is for Snape to favor the Slytherins. Hermione underhandedly helps Ron cheat during Quidditch tryouts in HBP so he can make the team, not to mention the fact that she does years of homework for him, which is why he never seems to learn anything. Then in the Epilogue, Ron brags about using magic to cheat on his Muggle driving test! So the Gryffindors don't seem to be glorious at all. Yet it's clear that Rowling wants us to pull for Gryffindor in spite of their flaws so that Harry can always win because he is so darn brave.

There are a few Gryffindors who aren't thrill seekers, such as Neville, Dean, Parvati, and Angelina. It's only when Neville gets covered with cuts and bruises, standing up to the Carrows and then Voldemort, that he finally seems worthy of Gryffindor house—even to readers who liked Neville all along anyway! It's as if all of us bought into the idea from the books that only the brave deserve praise, and everyone else can go hang. Even Neville's gran, who never seems to like him much before he becomes a warrior, suddenly respects him in DH. The motto of Gryffindor ought to be: "Be Reckless, Be Warlike—Go for the Glory."

Verdict

Are Gryffindors equal to those in other houses, or are they born in the winner's circle, destined for glorious triumphs? While posing for future statues could be seen as a Gryffindor trait, most of these characters have fallen off their pedestals by Book Seven. Verdict: No—while the focus is on the Gryffindors and their courage, they are not too glorified.

Which scene is funnier—Draco the bouncing ferret or the Weasley twins' fireworks show?

Draco as the Bouncing Ferret (GoF)

Professor Mad-Eye Moody is lurking around in the schoolyard, and he's aching to teach Draco a lesson. So when he hears the boy bragging about his Death-Eater father Lucius, and making fun of Harry's dead parents, the punishment is swift and hilarious. Moody brandishes his wand and Draco becomes a slinky white ferret that goes bouncing all around a school courtyard. Now that's what we call *cruel and unusual*. Would a real teacher do that? Is there a mystery here? Professor McGonagall comes to Draco's rescue, telling Moody off for abusing a ferret, that is to say, Draco. Priceless.

The Weasley Twins' Fireworks (OotP)

Fed up with detentions and Umbridge's evil black quill that writes in blood, Fred and George decide to use some magical fireworks to have a blast and get revenge. And it's real magic as they zoom around the hallways on broomsticks, tossing firebombs and even a huge flaming dragon that chases Umbridge right out of her classroom. At the end, all the kids in the school rush outside cheering to watch the Weasley brothers zoom away, leading to delivery of possibly the greatest quote in the entire book—"Give her hell from us, Peeves."

Verdict

These are all crowd-pleasing scenes, filled with perfect dramatic timing and incredible visuals. Moody helps Draco discover his inner ferret, and the Weasley twins completely own Umbridge and then fly away into the sunset. Which is funnier? Considering that one of us may (or may not) have actually jumped out of our chair and fist-pumped in the air after the Weasley twins' sendoff and Peeves' salute, the verdict has to be: We love Gred and Forge.

What is the best plotline in the books?

Snape: Good or Evil?

Severus Snape is a polarizing character—either you nearly love him or you want to murder him. This plotline of Snape being either good or evil runs throughout the series. It is cleverly set up so that at first he seems villainous because he's dressed in all black and we never know exactly what he is thinking or doing. What we do always know is that Harry has seething anger toward him. It's a persuasive viewpoint from our hero, which works as a very effective filter to make many readers see Snape as a heartless baddie beyond redemption (when really he was redeemed long before Harry came to Hogwarts according to his memories in DH).

J.K.R. also sets Snape up as the teacher from hell, hoping that readers won't notice when he tries to save Harry's (or someone's) life in nearly every book. In the first two books, Snape just seems to be a strict disciplinarian, and actually not that different from Professor McGonagall, who also keeps a tidy classroom and thinks Neville Longbottom is rather dense. But in PoA, Snape evolves into someone who seems to be picking on Harry all the time. It couldn't be that Snape would actually fear for Harry's life or want to protect him, could it? To the young teenage Harry, Snape is just trying to ruin his fun with the Marauder's Map, pouncing on Harry in the hallway every few minutes asking where he's going and what he's doing. By the time Snape charges into the Shrieking Shack at the end nearly frothing at the mouth with anger, readers don't know what to think or why he really has it in for Remus Lupin and Sirius Black. Harry sees it all as payback for some childhood grudge, and that's what J.K.R. wants us to think, but that's another diversion from the real truth.

As each book was released, J.K.R. was careful to leave out certain facts about Snape, even making sure that Dumbledore couldn't reveal his secrets to Harry. So readers would just roll their eyes along with Harry when

Dumbledore would say he trusted Snape but he couldn't explain why. How convenient. GoF added another layer to Snape's character, showing his encounters with an ex-Death Eater named Karkaroff and a suspicious Mad-Eye Moody. Dumbledore also sends Snape on a mysterious mission at the end. GoF finally opens the door to a possible Good Snape scenario, with Harry seeing Dumbledore testifying in the Pensieve that Snape had really come back to the good side when Harry was a baby, and had risked his life as a spy. At the end of the book, Snape rushes in to rescue Harry once again alongside Dumbledore and McGonagall, and all three of them appear in Death Eater Barty Crouch, Jr.'s Foe Glass, a sign that they were all three on Harry's side.

So J.K.R. was almost spelling out the truth, but many readers were fed up with Snape by then. In GoF, he is unkind to Hermione about her teeth when they grow to beaver size after a jinx hits her; Snape also gives Neville a detention disemboweling toads, which seems over-the-top even for Snape. But fans should try to look at these scenes a different way because there is some sly humor going on. In the case of Hermione and the oversized teeth, Snape is comparing her to Goyle, who has also been hexed with pustules all over his face. So, Snape is just telling the truth when he says he sees no difference between Goyle and Hermione in how badly the two students are jinxed. Or Snape might be playing down how big Hermione's teeth really are to make her feel better, but J.K.R. makes him say it completely backward so readers take it the wrong way. Or maybe Hermione is more hurt that Pansy Parkinson and her gang are laughing at her teeth? As for Neville cutting up the toads, is that any worse than a Muggle biology class? Later on in DH, Neville does some major dissecting on Voldemort's snake when he cuts off its head! So Snape might have just been giving Neville the right skills after all. Actually, Snape really isn't any worse than Professor Flitwick, who in HBP gives Seamus Finnigan an insulting line to write for detention: "I am a wizard not a baboon brandishing a stick" [HBP, p. 355]. Harry doesn't get angry with Flitwick for that punishment, but he is always furious at Snape, and that extends the idea that Snape is evil.

In OotP and HBP, Snape remains on the outs with Harry, even though Harry feels pity when he sees some of Snape's childhood memories of being bullied by Harry's father and Sirius Black. Since Snape and Sirius never got along, Harry continues to blame Snape for the death of Sirius in HBP because Harry enjoys believing it was Snape. It is Kreacher, though, who betrays Sirius, and Bellatrix Lestrange who pushes him through the Veil of Death. Again, as readers, we are supposed to blame Snape too, and to always agree with Harry. As HBP goes along, Harry becomes more and more convinced that Snape fits right in with Voldemort and the Death Eaters, and Draco amazingly shares his opinion. They both think Snape is a double spy for the Dark Side, and by the time Snape kills Dumbledore at the end of HBP, nearly every reader is wondering if that is true.

So the huge question going into DH was whether Snape was good or evil, and some fans were unhappy because they felt that Snape's story had almost become bigger than Harry's own story. Many wondered why J.K.R. wasted so much page space on this hateful dark Death Eater who taught school but hated kids, and they figured it might turn out that Harry was going to kill him on page one of DH. Even fans of Professor Snape did not feel totally secure in the belief that Snape was good or that he would be cleared of the murder of Dumbledore, and many wondered how the hints of Snape's love for Harry's mother might play a part in the final book.

It was an obsession on both sides, and the final book still kept readers in suspense until later chapters when it was finally revealed that Snape was much more complex than he seemed, and that he never wanted Dumbledore or Harry dead. And guess what? Harry has to reverse many of his earlier opinions because Snape does so many things to help Harry that vastly outweigh the classroom dramas and detentions. Seen through adult eyes, Snape is redeemed before Harry is even born, and he is always on the good side due to his love for Lily Potter. He cares about Dumbledore, and he carries out his mission to help Harry. Few characters in the books are actually as good as Snape, in spite of his outward appearance and rough language. It's not a surprise that on the second-to-the-last page of DH, Harry is still talking about Snape, saying he was the bravest man he ever knew, and there's no question anymore that Snape was a good guy. Fans are still talking about Snape, too, and the debate continues.

Search for the Horcruxes

Unlike the plotline about the three Deathly Hallows, the story of Voldemort's Horcruxes is much easier to follow and starts back in SS, Chapter One, when Professor McGonagall asks Dumbledore about baby Harry's scar. Why can't Dumbledore heal Harry's famous lightning-bolt scar? Well, we find out later that it has a Horcrux inside, a bit of Voldemort's unstable soul that shattered and attached itself to Harry's head as a baby. Readers see Horcruxes and don't even know it—Tom Riddle's diary, for instance in CoS, which holds a bit of his younger self. So in HBP, when Dumbledore explains why he wants to teach Harry the story of Tom Riddle/Lord Voldemort's life, it suddenly makes sense that the Dark Lord has a way to survive outside of his body. Each Horcrux holds a torn bit of Voldemort's soul trapped inside, and is protected by a curse.

And even though Harry has to shift between the Deathly Hallows and the Horcruxes in DH, it's obvious that Voldemort will only be truly dead once every single Horcrux is shattered. Harry destroys Tom Riddle's diary in CoS, while Dumbledore shatters the Peverell ring in HBP. Harry must track down Helga Hufflepuff's cup, Salazar Slytherin's locket, and Rowena Ravenclaw's diadem. The final three Horcruxes are inside living beings: Nagini the snake, Harry, and Voldemort himself. Harry is the eighth Horcrux.

Yes, it's a quest and a treasure hunt, but the best part of the Horcrux plotline is the moral weight of it. It's about a murderer ripping apart his own soul to become immortal, and diminishing his human side instead, as Dumbledore explains in HBP. Voldemort, with his snaky face and red eyes, just isn't human anymore, either in looks or emotions. Harry has to come to terms with his mind's connection to a vicious killer in DH, and then learn to use the visions he sees through his own Horcrux for good instead of evil. The plotline is also about the way people's souls can be painfully repaired through remorse, as if being alive is one big fix-it project and only good works can put someone back together again. It's a traditionally Christian view of redemption through good works, but also a universal view of human transformation.

Verdict

In a long epic story like Harry Potter, the plotlines are intricate, profound, and sweeping. Can we really know whether someone is good or evil just by looking at them, as with Severus Snape? And what does evil do to the human soul, especially when murder is involved? Verdict: Trying to figure out whose side Snape was really on kept us on our toes throughout the whole series. It's gotta be the best plotline.

Does the Secret-Keeper information revealed in Deathly Hallows *contradict the previous rules about Secret-Keepers?*

Yes!

Secret-Keepers are made when a Fidelius Charm is placed on someone or something to make it/them invisible to all but the chosen Secret-Keeper. The facts about the Fidelius Charm, however, become much more complicated in DH, thanks to new information that seems to contradict earlier books. Readers thought they understood how the charm worked from Professor Flitwick who says in PoA:

> [The Fidelius Charm is] an immensely complex spell involving the magical concealment of a secret inside a single, living soul. The information is hidden inside the chosen person, or Secret-Keeper, and is henceforth impossible to find—unless, of course, the Secret-Keeper chooses to divulge it. [PoA, p. 205]

A few years later, the author answered a fan question on her official site about "What happens when a Secret-Keeper dies?"

> When a Secret-Keeper dies, their secret dies with them, or, to put it another way, the status of their secret will remain as it was at the moment of their death. Everybody in whom they confided will continue to know the hidden information, but nobody else. [JKR-OS]

And all of that made sense. Peter Pettigrew was the Potters' Secret-Keeper and when he told Voldemort their location, he could go there, enter the house, and kill the family (he failed to kill Harry, of course). That's the reason Sirius wanted to kill Peter after the death of James and Lily, since he knew that only Peter could be the traitor. Sirius knew where the Potters were in Godric's Hollow, but he couldn't tell anyone, since he wasn't the Secret-Keeper.

And again, in OotP, Dumbledore was the Secret-Keeper for Grimmauld Place, and the only way Harry could see the address of the house was when Mad-Eye Moody showed him a piece of paper written by Dumbledore himself. No paper—no entry. It was very clear that anyone who could get into the Order of the Phoenix Headquarters found out the address directly from Dumbledore and nobody else. But Dumbledore died at the end of HBP, and that meant that only the people who had known about Grimmauld Place before could get in. The secret died with him. . . or did it?

In DH, J.K.R. introduces an entirely new spin on the Fidelius Charm, and it's almost the opposite of what we understood before. Arthur Weasley tells the kids that because Dumbledore died, every survivor of the Order of the Phoenix has become a Secret-Keeper and the Fidelius Charm is breaking down. So instead of one Secret-Keeper, Grimmauld Place suddenly has twenty Secret-Keepers. *What?* Why would the spell work that way? That is the opposite of keeping a secret, and goes against what the spell is meant to do, which is to protect others from finding out the secret.

The only answer is that J.K.R. needed to change the spell to fit the plotline she had in mind. But it's hard to believe she expected the readers to buy it. It's just totally inconsistent. For instance, in DH, the kids can go back to Grimmauld Place to hide because they already know the address from before Dumbledore died. But when a Death Eater named Yaxley grabs Hermione's arm and Apparates with her to the door, where he can see the address too, the rules get complicated. That shouldn't happen under the old rules of the Fidelius Charm. Because of Hermione's fear that Yaxley and the other Death Eaters are going to invade Grimmauld Place, the Order loses their safe house and suddenly the kids have to go on an extended camping trip, which is all J.K.R. wants them to do. So the new Secret-Keeper information is just a plot device to move the action away from Grimmauld Place. But it's also a plot hole because the Trio never considers doing something simple, such as redoing the Fidelius Charm to make Harry the new Secret-Keeper so they can stay at Grimmauld Place. Hermione should have thought of that.

And then we come to the muddled plotline about Shell Cottage, home to Bill and Fleur Weasley. Bill Weasley makes himself Secret-Keeper for his own home (a brilliant idea that never occurs to James or Lily Potter), so only Bill can give someone the address. Yet for some unknown reason, Ron is able to tell the address to Dobby: "Shell Cottage on the outskirts of Tinworth" [DH, p. 468]. That's not right at all. Ron isn't the Secret-Keeper of Shell Cottage, and even if he knows the location, he can't divulge it, right? That's the reason Snape cannot tell Bellatrix about Grimmauld Place in *Half-Blood Prince*:

> I am not the Secret-Keeper; I cannot speak the name of the
> place. You understand how the enchantment works, I think?
> [HBP, p. 30]

In HBP, Dumbledore has to visit the Dursleys in person to give them the address of Grimmauld Place, because *only he is the Secret-Keeper*. But Bill Weasley inexplicably goes on to tell Harry that the rest of his family is at Aunt Muriel's house, and Arthur is the Secret-Keeper there. Again, only Arthur should have been able to say that, or to write it down. Whoops!

No!

Wrong—there is no contradiction with the Fidelius Charm. It is unfair to compare what J.K.R. wrote on her website with the books themselves. But even so, J.K.R. was right because after Dumbledore's death, the secret remained the same and no one new could be allowed into Grimmauld Place. Anyone who knew the address of Grimmauld Place when Dumbledore was alive would still know it, and that's exactly what we have in DH. All the Order Members share the knowledge, so they all become new Secret-Keepers.

And if Hermione is able to lead Yaxley to the door, then that is J.K.R.'s way of telling us that there are loopholes in the Fidelius Charm. There are ways to get inside a secret place if the magic isn't strong enough, and Mr. Weasley says the magic is getting weaker. Why is this confusing? Flitwick never talked about that possibility in PoA because it never came up, but it still could have been true. Even in OotP, the members were worried about spies and being followed home. That's why Harry was escorted everywhere, such as with the Advanced Guard? Dumbledore even said in HBP that Grimmauld Place might not stay Unplottable once Sirius was dead, and that Bellatrix might show up to claim inheritance of it; only the house-elf Kreacher could stop her by being loyal to Harry. Why would Dumbledore be worried about that since he was the only Secret-Keeper? That's proof right there that certain things can weaken a Fidelius Charm.

When Ron tells Dobby the address of Shell Cottage, perhaps Bill has not put the charm on his house yet. It is only after Harry and a bunch of wounded people Apparate on his doorstep that Bill realizes he needs extra protection. Bill also doesn't give anyone Aunt Muriel's exact address, but only mentions her name and her house. So, hey, no problem. J.K.R. hasn't contradicted anything, and all is well with the Fidelius Charm.

Verdict

Were the rules of the Fidelius Charm changed in Deathly Hallows to help the plot keep moving along? Or, is this a case of nitpicky readers who can't accept new information about an old charm? Until J.K.R. clears up the secrets of Secret Keeping, the verdict is: Oh yeah—the new Secret-Keeper information completely contradicts the old.

Which movie did a worse job capturing the important details of the book?

In these movies, the choices made by the studios of what to exclude diminishes the story, and sometimes the spotlight is on the wrong characters.

Order of the Phoenix

Several problems make OotP the least true-to-the-story movie, and to anyone who has read the book, it's noticeable right away. Mrs. Figg is there, but not Mundungus Fletcher, so the humor that balances the attack of the Dementor in the book is lacking. At the Dursleys, it's the same old thing with Petunia taking Dudley's side against Harry, but sadly missing is the big scene in which Petunia has to admit she knows about the wizarding world—she never gets the Howler message from Dumbledore that says "Remember my last!" reminding her that she must protect Harry. Professor Lupin is missing from the Advanced Guard scene, and it would have been much better to see him and Tonks together from the beginning. As it is, David Thewlis's character seems almost an afterthought in the movie, and he hardly has any lines. Ron, unfortunately, misses his big Quidditch moment, because the whole "Weasley is our King" subplot isn't in there.

While the studios warned us that this movie would be "dark," no one knew they were talking about the murky lighting. Except for Umbridge's pink office and Luna Lovegood's Spectrespecs, every scene appears filtered through a blue lens: dark skies, dark tunnels, dark houses, dark forest, dark dungeons—even Dumbledore's office looks darker than it did in earlier movies. Grimmauld Place is drab, except for one glimpse of the Black Tapestry. Where are the snaky Slytherin light fixtures? Or the cupboards full of dangerous objects? Kreacher the house-elf turns out strangely cute instead of ugly, and we never see his "lair" under the boiler. Fans were looking forward to seeing Mrs. Black's portrait, but it remains covered up with no shrieking.

And once the kids are at Hogwarts, Dolores Umbridge takes over the plot. The actress Imelda Staunton plays her evil role with glee, but after a while she wears out her welcome with her shrill voice and pink costumes. The focus on Umbridge is just wrong because the filmmakers played down her counterpoint, Severus Snape, played passionately by Alan Rickman in one good scene. In the book, the ironic twist is that Dolores, with her little girl giggle, is the monster while the dark and moody Snape is working for the Order of the Phoenix. But half of Snape's scenes are cut. Instead of a big showdown about Harry with Sirius Black, we barely hear them talking through the kitchen door for just a second. There is no Potions class in which Snape makes sure that Harry knows how to brew the Draught of Peace. Instead, it becomes just another Umbridge scene, with Snape hitting Ron on the head for comedy. Snape tries to protect Harry's mind from the Dark Lord through Occlumency, and though that one scene captures Snape and Harry's rocky relationship, most of it has been shredded on the cutting room floor. Harry sees only flashes of "Snape's Worst Memory" of being bullied by the Marauders, and there is no Lily Evans to come to his defense. It's apparently more important to the filmmakers to waste money on Umbridge with giants and centaurs than to develop a truly important character like Snape.

And the worst problem of all is the death of Sirius Black. The duel at the Ministry is swashbuckling, and Gary Oldman's Sirius has a great time fighting off Lucius Malfoy (Jason Isaacs). But why does Sirius have to call Harry "James" at the very last minute? That's not in the book, and if they had to make that point, it should have come much earlier in the movie. And why does the Veil of Death look like an old set from *Star Trek*? We didn't expect a shower curtain, but it's supposed to be a "Veil of Death" and not smoky clouds. Then after Sirius dies, Harry's heart-to-heart talk with Dumbledore is cut down to a few lines, and there's no emotional tantrum or discussion of the prophecy, which is the real climax in the book. Thus there is no payoff for viewers to see how much Harry is suffering before he goes off to have pudding with Luna. It's a lame ending to a watered-down movie that should have been less about politics and more about people.

Goblet of Fire

While there are some truly memorable performances in GoF, including David Tennant as Barty Crouch, Jr. and Brendan Gleason as Mad-Eye Moody, the movie flounders around and doesn't do justice to the book. It's not exactly bad, but there are so many subplots that the movie can't capture them all. For instance, we see both Barty Crouch Senior and Junior in the Pensieve and in the present, but there is no way to explain in the movie that Barty's father is a hypocrite who sprung him from jail. A few words from Winky the house-elf would have helped, but she was written out, as was Hermione's interest in house-elf rights and S.P.E.W. It's too bad that the theme of overcoming prejudice was written out.

The Quidditch World Cup is a big deal, but much too short. Then later, far too much time is spent on the Yule Ball, which is just a showcase for the teen actors. The fight with the dragon goes much longer than in the book. The maze in the Third Task is missing so many great elements that it is a big disappointment. Fans wanted to see the Sphinx, the giant spider, and the Blast-Ended Skrewt come to life. As it is, the champions are just jumping around in the shrubbery.

Character development isn't that strong in this movie, and key scenes with Severus Snape and Sirius Black are left out. There's no confrontation at the end with Snape showing Cornelius Fudge his Dark Mark, for instance, and no meeting with Padfoot at the local cave to discuss the Death Eaters. Yet a silly scene with Rita Skeeter is included, and while Miranda Richardson plays the character to the hilt, her character goes nowhere. The subplot about Rita being an Animagus beetle who eavesdrops on people was deleted. And so much time and money is spent on the weird bathtub scene with Moaning Myrtle—come on! Who cares about that egg anyway?

Ralph Fiennes is creepy and cool as the returning Voldemort, and Michael Gambon does a pretty good job with Cedric Diggory's eulogy. But Emma Watson's line about "Everything's going to change now, isn't it?" is a really lame ending.

Verdict

The directors of Goblet of Fire *chose to run with special effects and focus on certain characters while leaving out some that were dear to the fans.* Order of the Phoenix *has a similar problem with too much importance given to Professor Umbridge, and not enough to Snape's memories. Which is the worst? While there are problems with GoF, Warner Bros. gutted the heart out of OotP when Snape's memories were tossed. Verdict:* Order of the Phoenix *is the movie that truly fails to capture the book's important details.*

Are Harry and Hermione partly responsible for Snape's death since they never tried to save his life?

No!

There was nothing Harry and Hermione could do to save Snape's life. Snape's fate was sealed the moment the Dark Lord had him in the Shrieking Shack trapped with Nagini the giant snake. He was at Voldemort's mercy, and if either of the kids had raised a wand to zap Voldemort, they both might have died, and the snake would still have been there to kill Snape. Harry thinks about trying to kill Nagini, but he's not sure he can do it. And he doesn't automatically step in to help Snape because he still believes that Snape is Dumbledore's murderer.

Nagini has poisonous venom that nearly kills Arthur Weasley in OotP because the wounds won't heal properly [OotP, p. 507]. Snape is bitten more severely than Arthur and right in the throat over an artery, so the poison enters his bloodstream so quickly there is nothing they can do. Even after Voldemort leaves Harry and Hermione alone with Snape, no amount of dittany herb would have stopped the bleeding, so of course they are not to blame. It was Snape's time to die, and he accepted that.

Yes!

Harry and Hermione are brave Gryffindor wizards with magical powers, so of course it's their fault that they didn't lift a wand to help Snape survive. Every other time Harry has seen someone die he always felt a need to help them and be a hero, but this time he suddenly doesn't? He liberated the Muggle-borns from the Ministry, a dragon from Gringotts, and Draco and Goyle from the burning Room of Requirement, but for Snape he does nothing? Why does he forget that Snape equals the Half-Blood Prince, the boy from the *Potions Book* whom he had thought of as a friend? Why does he forget all the times Dumbledore said he trusted Snape? Maybe Harry can be partly forgiven, since at one point he suddenly views Snape's death through the raging mind-connection with Voldemort. But what about Hermione? She never hated Snape in spite of her problems with him, and when he was knocked out in PoA, she was quite worried about him.

So what could they have done? Well, first of all, Disapparation—they could have disappeared and reappeared elsewhere. We are told several times in *Prisoner of Azkaban* that the Shrieking Shack, where Snape's death occurs, is not on the Hogwarts grounds where Disapparation doesn't work, but in Hogsmeade, where it does. Even if there were charms on the Shack to keep Lupin in, when Dumbledore died those probably disappeared, because most magical spells are broken in the books upon death. And since Harry and Hermione escaped using Disapparation from Grimmauld Place, the Lovegood house, and Bathilda's house, then why not the Shack? They could have blown a hole in the wall, as Snape did earlier when he fled from McGonagall, and flown Snape right out of there.

And secondly, what about a Freezing Charm on the snake? Immobilus, perhaps? Or they could have tried a combination Leg-Lock and Stupefy on Voldemort. What about those silent spells they learned in HBP, which Harry uses to great effect later on in the battle? Or the biggie—Shield Charm, anyone? Harry protects nearly everyone with that just a few chapters after Snape dies. Even *Expelliarmus* would have forced Voldemort's wand out of his hand—are Harry and Hermione brain dead? Haven't they used that spell in the Shack together before? Hello? It's frustrating because Harry actually has the loyalty of the Elder Wand at that point and Voldemort couldn't have killed him. Of course, Harry and Hermione are responsible for not helping Snape.

Verdict

Did Harry and Hermione owe Snape any help in the Shrieking Shack, or were they wise to lay low as bystanders when the snake attacked? Should they have tried a diversion—made a few old chairs fly at Voldemort, perhaps? Or use some first-year spells or at least Muggle first aid? They had no moral obligation to endanger their lives to save the life of someone whom they justifiably assumed was Dumbledore's murderer. Verdict: No, they shouldn't be held responsible.

Which couple has the most romantic story?

Harry/Ginny

It's obvious from the beginning that Ginny is the Princess to Harry's Prince Charming after he rescues her from the dragon, that is to say, basilisk, in CoS. Even before that, they meet at King's Cross Station in SS, which is not only Harry's heavenly place in DH, but also the place where J.K.R. says on her official site that her own parents met and started their life together. Of course, for most of the series Harry is clueless about birds and bees or Ginny's shy feelings toward him, expressed by the anonymous valentine that began with the sincere but unflattering "Eyes as green as a fresh pickled toad" [CoS, p. 238].

But Ginny's affection for Harry is timeless, and after managing to push all other girls out of the way with her Quidditch broom, she finally gets Harry's attention in HBP. It might have helped that Harry was sniffing Amortentia love potion fumes for half of the book, but whatever—once the sweet scent of honeysuckle wafts his way, he only has green-pickled eyes for Ginny. Their first kiss, or "snog" if you prefer, is in front of the entire Gryffindor Common Room in HBP, and after that, their love knows no bounds. Soon Ginny is so sure of their relationship that she teases other girls about Harry's macho tattoo of a Hungarian horntail, as if he really has one. When Cho Chang tries to flirt again in DH, Ginny is there to just say a big NO, and since she has the flashing eyes and red hair of Harry's dreams, he has to obey [DH, p. 585]. After a lonely separation during Voldiewar II, when Harry can only watch Ginny's name moving around on the Marauder's Map, they survive to live Happily Ever After with their three adorable little Potters in the Epilogue of DH. What's more romantic than that?

Ron/Hermione

These two get off to a rocky start, not helped by the fact Ron locked Hermione in the girl's restroom in SS with a giant mountain troll when they were eleven. But, of course, that's why, in the long run, their love is the essence of childhood romance. The bickering and shouting is a sign of their own unique chemistry, and it takes them a long time to grow up and solve their problems. Even so, Ron nearly loses his chance when he forgets to invite Hermione to the Yule Ball in GoF. He can't quite sort out whether his jealousy toward Viktor Krum is about losing the girl or merely Quidditch envy. Even in HBP, when most of the kids are paired off, Ron is still oblivious to Hermione's feelings, and starts messing around in dark corners with Lavender Brown. How could he be so dense? Sometimes true love takes many detours, as in HBP when Ron chomps down a bunch of Chocolate Cauldrons laced with love potion from Romilda Vane, or in the same book when Hermione goes on a hot revenge date with the hulking Cormac McLaggan.

Their darkest hour together is in DH, when Ron seems to be gone forever, leaving Hermione sobbing in her tent for days. But, Eureka! Ron realizes that Dumbledore's Deluminator was a heart-light that can lead him back to the one he loves best, and he finds Hermione again. After both of them help Harry save the wizarding world, the lovebirds settle down together to bicker and argue their way through parenthood and whatever else life has to offer. It's a romantic tale as old as time.

Harry/Hermione

Despite a considerable amount of waffling from the author in the last few books in the series, events in the final book appeared, *to the untrained eye*, to settle all disputes concerning the romantic loyalties of Harry and Hermione once and for all.

In reality, the evidence so far has been somewhat mixed. Harry and Hermione's passionate love for each other—platonically disguised for years—has created a series of powerful bonds between them. Those trained in the art of deception will recognize Jo's blatant decoys in the Epilogue for what they are—pure, unwashed disguise. However, watchful fans see the endgame: Fate will intervene and J.K.R.'s giant smokescreen will be revealed.

Ron is likely to have a midlife crisis and divorce boring Hermione. Ginny is way too hot for Harry—she'll probably have an affair with some hot young wizard, which will break up their awkward and hastily arranged marriage. Then, finally, destiny will have the last laugh and the most beautiful love story ever told will reach its magnificent climax as the two embrace as lovers for the first time

Verdict

Ginny's passionate but clueless love object had a lot to learn, but Ginny was willing to wait until Harry saw her as the girl of his dreams. Ron took his own sweet time asking Hermione to go steady, but eventually made himself worthy of her love. Harry and Hermione were the lead roles in the greatest love story never told. Which story is most romantic? The Hero and the Princess? The Sidekick and the Brain? The Lucky Guy and the Nerd? Verdict: Ron and Hermione had more problems, but also more passion, and that makes them the most romantic.

Who would win in a fight: centaurs or giants?

Centaurs

This is like saying who's smarter: Hermione or Stan Shunpike? It's obvious that centaurs are about one hundred IQ points higher in intelligence than the giants, so it should be easy for them to win a fight. With their knowledge of stars and the future, centaurs could figure the odds of winning the battle, and choose the best time to attack. They are fast on their hooves, and can easily dodge the giants' big feet. While it's true that they mostly anger Hagrid's brother Grawp with their bows and arrows, working together, the herd could use ropes to bring a giant down and then stomp him with their horseshoes. Also, giants are bloodthirsty toward their own kind, which is why there are so few of them left. The centaurs could just start a fight between several giants, and let them kill each other.

Giants

Centaurs could never win a battle with giants. The size factor is what matters, and Grawp was able to knock down a centaur with a wave of his big beefy hand, and he wasn't even trying. A giant is like a one-man army, able to rip a tall pine tree out of the ground. So one giant could take out a whole regiment of centaurs with one swipe of his tree club, and there's nothing the centaurs could do except run away.

Verdict

In the battle between centaurs and giants, would the key be brains or brawn? Centaurs like to believe that they are superior in all things, but the fact is the giants could crush them like animal crackers. The giants would definitely have the strength advantage, but these buffoons would be no match for the collective brain power of the centaurs in large numbers. Verdict: The ratio of centaurs to giants would determine the victor.

Besides Voldemort, who is the worst villain?

Lucius Malfoy

For most of the series, Lucius Malfoy is Voldemort's right-hand man. A snobby pureblood, Lucius sneers at anyone he feels is beneath him, which is almost everyone. Ask his house-elf Dobby, who has to iron his hands daily for punishment. While Lucius loves his own son, he never hesitates to threaten the Weasleys and Harry, and his scheming puts everyone in danger. It's Lucius who gives eleven-year-old Ginny the haunted Horcrux diary of Tom Riddle in CoS, unleashing the basilisk into Hogwarts. In PoA, he tries to get Dumbledore fired as headmaster, and convinces the Ministry to behead Buckbeak the hippogriff. His sinister plot to get the prophecy orb in OotP leads to the death of Sirius Black, his own wife's cousin. Even after spending time in Azkaban in HBP, Lucius comes crawling back to the Dark Lord, handing over his home and his wand in DH. Maybe Lucius shows a glimmer of remorse in the end when he thinks he has lost Draco, but his good behavior probably won't last very long.

Fenrir Greyback

The word beast really fits Fenrir Greyback, the hideous werewolf who just can't wait for a full moon to feast on his victims. While not a Death Eater, Fenrir works for Voldemort as an attack dog, killing or maiming anyone who won't cooperate with the Dark Lord. He preys on small children, contaminating them so they will grow up to be part of his werewolf army. He bit and turned Remus Lupin into a werewolf as a child, scratched and scarred Bill Weasley with wounds that won't heal, and mercilessly tortured Hermione at Malfoy Manor. Easily recognized by his foul stench and bloodstained clothes, not to mention excessive body hair, Fenrir is really just a watered-down version of Voldemort—a Slytherin in wolf's clothing.

Verdict

Lucius is an aristocrat able to pull strings at the Ministry for his evil purposes. Fenrir is a hired thug with cannibalistic tendencies. Which one is almost equal to the Dark Lord? For all his pureblood bravado, Lucius fails as a henchman. Living the glamorous life at Malfoy Manor has made him too soft. Verdict: The stinky Fenrir Greyback is the next-best villain to Voldemort.

Should Parseltongue be taught at Hogwarts?

Yes!

If Ron can learn enough Parseltongue to open the Chamber of Secrets in DH, then why shouldn't it be taught as a magical language at Hogwarts? Kids wouldn't find the sound of snake language so threatening if they understood the grammar and accents. What better way to show house unity than to help the other three houses understand a particularly Slytherin skill? And it could be really useful if someone were threatened again by a roving basilisk or maverick Ashwinder. Beyond the obvious extermination purposes, the Healers at St. Mungo's could ask a snake's permission to milk venom for antidotes. Maybe Voldemort had a few good ideas after all.

No!

It's truly insane to think that anyone would want to take a class in Parseltongue. Harry doesn't exactly enjoy the talent, and it just about ruins his reputation at Hogwarts—all the Hufflepuffs start hiding from him. Witches and wizards are never going to forget that Voldemort was a Parselmouth, so why would they want their kids to be like him? Making slithery sounds is creepy, and snakes are dangerous. What if someone died while practicing their homework? As for Ron, he merely mimics Harry to open the Chamber of Secrets, and doesn't really know what he is saying. In the Epilogue, he warns his own children *not* to become Slytherins or he will disown them. It's a surefire bet he wouldn't want them to study Parseltongue.

Verdict

Should the hissing begin in Parseltongue 101 Class? Or would parents have a hissy fit if their children spoke to snakes? Verdict: It's time for the houses to cease squabbling, and to sincerely study Parseltongue, the whispery speech of sinuous snakes.

Do the life debts really matter?

Yes!

Every act of mercy in which somebody's life is saved matters in the final analysis because it sets up a life debt in which the "saved" owe their "savior" a major favor. It isn't magic like the Unbreakable Vow, but it is important. Harry saves Dudley's soul from the Dementors in OotP, and his cousin is grateful for that in DH. Snape owes at least two life debts: one to James Potter for saving him from the werewolf, and the other to Dumbledore for sparing his life and letting him join the Order of the Phoenix. Because of all the accumulated life debt, Snape protects Harry at Hogwarts and does whatever Dumbledore asks of him. Harry in his turn keeps Sirius from killing Peter, who strangles himself instead of harming Harry and Ron in DH.

There are more subtle life debts going on, too. Dumbledore offers to help Draco and Narcissa before he dies in HBP, which may have been why in DH Draco doesn't want to identify Harry and Hermione to his father at Malfoy Manor. Harry frees Dobby from the Malfoys, and there's no doubt that Dobby returns the favor by saving the entire group before he dies. Life debts basically drive the whole story.

No!

Life debts aren't magically binding at all—that's just a lie Dumbledore tells Harry in SS because he can't expose Snape's secret love for Lily. As for Peter, how does he return Harry's mercy? He goes along with the plan in GoF to trap Harry in the graveyard, kills Cedric Diggory, cuts off his own arm to help Voldemort return, and then stands by while Harry is tortured. That's not paying a life debt! The fact that Peter strangles himself in DH is more about his wicked silver hand turning on him than him thinking about doing something good. Peter loses his free will long before that.

Most of the characters help others out of loyalty, love, and choosing good over evil, and those are better themes than being trapped in a life debt for the rest of your life.

Verdict

In the accounting book of life, were Snape and Pettigrew magically indebted to others? Or were life debts a big zero in the reciprocal mercy equation? Verdict: Loyalty and love added up with the life debts, so they really do matter.

Is the Snitch worth too many points in Quidditch?

Yes!

When a Seeker catches the Golden Snitch it ends the game and gives the team one hundred and fifty extra points. That is *far* too many points. Quidditch is supposed to be a team sport, so the scoring is unfair to Chasers, who only get ten points for a goal even when they are dodging Bludgers. Beaters and Keepers work just as hard, but don't score any points at all. And all they can really hope to do for most of the game is keep the other team's Chasers from scoring mostly worthless goals. Because the rest of the time the action on the field is irrelevant, the Seeker isn't just the most valuable player—the Seeker is the *only* player. The game may as well be a giant Easter egg hunt—with one egg.

No!

Fair is fair, and if the Seeker has enough skill to catch the Golden Snitch while flying at top speed, then that team deserves to win the most points. The Chasers are just lucky the goals for the Quaffles are worth ten points, instead of two as in Muggle basketball. And games have to go on and on until the Snitch is caught, but that doesn't *always* mean the team will win. At the Quidditch World Cup in GoF, Ireland has more points for goals, so when Krum catches the Snitch, Bulgaria loses the match even with one hundred and fifty points. That time the Chasers ruled instead of the Seeker. And anyway, Beaters can hit Bludgers at the other team's Seeker! There's nothing wrong with Quidditch scoring at all.

Verdict

Can Quidditch ever be labeled a team sport with the outcome of virtually every game decided by the same player? Or is Quidditch a balanced sport with rules that have withstood the test of time? Verdict: The Snitch is worth too much in Quidditch. Way, way *too much.*

Would you rather have Harry's Invisibility Cloak or his Firebolt flying broomstick?

Invisibility Cloak

Anyone would love to have Harry's Invisibility Cloak, his best protection and family heirloom. It's a fun way to sneak out to explore the opposite sex's Quidditch locker rooms, or to visit the Hogwarts kitchens for a snack. But, of course, this is no ordinary cloak—it is one of the three Deathly Hallows created by one of the Peverell brothers, meaning it is indestructible. You could use the cloak for undercover work, spying, or just keeping a low profile. All Muggles and even most wizards can't see through it, but watch out for really smart kneazle-cats and guys with creepy magic eyeballs.

Firebolt

Harry's favorite broom will take you anywhere you want to go, and you'll still be invisible to Muggles as long as they don't look up. Accelerating 0-150 miles per hour, this broom is super-fast, and you can learn all the fancy turns, dips, and dives that Harry uses during a Quidditch match. And you won't crash the way Harry did on his Nimbus Two Thousand, because the Firebolt has a nifty auto-brake. Just say "*Accio Firebolt!*" and even a flying dragon can't stop you.

Verdict

Would it be more fun to pull a disappearing act under the Cloak of Invisibility or to streak away like greased lightning on the Firebolt? The Firebolt is quite sexy, being the fastest broom in the world—but this Invisibility Cloak is truly one-of-a-kind. Verdict: Take the Cloak!

Who would be the scariest mom: Rita Skeeter or Dolores Umbridge?

Rita Skeeter

Imagine the fear of a helpless infant looking up and seeing the face of Rita Skeeter, buzzing around with her three gold teeth and beetle-eyed glasses. She would be the type of mother to write an embarrassing weekly column about her offspring's bed-wetting, nightmares, and problems at school. Forget about knitting sweaters or baking cookies, she wouldn't hesitate to dump her child with a house-elf and fly off to annoy the celebrities on the red carpet. In the child's teenage years, Rita would probably show her motherly love by "bugging" the kid's bedroom, reading diaries, and making sure the school yearbook gets the baby pictures. Don't worry—for revenge, her child can grow up and write a tell-all book about her.

Dolores Umbridge

It's frightening just to imagine this monster passing her genes on to the next generation. But one thing is certain: Whether it's a boy or a girl, the nursery is going to be decorated in pink. And cats—the kids will have cat books, cat toys, cat dishes, and probably have to learn to eat cat kibble. It's a remote possibility that motherhood might change Dolores for the better, as long as Little Precious Snooky-Ookums learns to obey and conform at an early age. Hem-Hem. Giggle! Quick! Call social services!

Verdict

Neither one of these women will ever win Witch Weekly's *Mother of the Year contest. Would it be worse to have Rita put your whole childhood on a flashing billboard in Diagon Alley? Or would you rather have years of hideous home-*

schooling with Dolores, trapped in a pink nightmare? Rita might verbally abuse her children in the press, but her Quick-Quotes Quill actually contains ink, unlike Dolores with her black quill of doom. Verdict: Dolores is scary enough to stunt a child's growth.

Should goblins and house-elves be allowed to carry wands?

No!

Goblins and house-elves do powerful magic without wands, so why do they need them? Besides, the elves have already shown that they couldn't care less. Hermione is convinced they want wands when she starts S.P.E.W. (Society for the Promotion of Elfish Welfare) in GoF, but her mission fails because the elves are content with their lowly status. Plus, they would have to be educated—in GoF, Winky swears she doesn't know how to use a wand when she is accused of casting the Dark Mark in GoF. Dobby sure as hell doesn't need a wand to blast Lucius away in CoS, or to disarm Narcissa in *Deathly Hallows*, when he shatters a crystal chandelier on top of his former masters.

As for goblins, while they may resent the wand-carrying wizards, they are already capable of making powerful weapons like the Sword of Gryffindor. Arming the nasty little blighters with wands too would just set up another goblin rebellion, which is the reason the Ministry banned wands from other creatures in the first place. Imagine what an angry goblin might do with the power of the Elder Wand? Society is safer when only humans know wandlore.

Yes!

Why shouldn't house-elves and goblins carry wands? Sure, they can already do magic, but so can many wizards before they have wands (think Harry and Lily). A wand is just a tool that focuses the inner magic. For the wizarding world to deny them wands and live in fear of them is a terrible prejudice that assumes the worst.

Nothing will ever change if wizards continue to be so close-minded. The magical community ignores the potential benefits of allowing these creatures use of a wand. Since house-elves can Apparate anywhere, and goblins know so much about metallurgy, perhaps they would share their knowledge if wizards would give them wands. It seems difficult to imagine young house-elves and goblins going to Ollivander's for wands and then taking classes at Hogwarts—but Hermione would sure love it!

Verdict

Human beings have a nearly impossible time understanding each other—much less an entirely different species. There are plenty of people in the magical world who can't be trusted with wands (*cough*Death Eaters*cough*). While trying to afford house-elves and goblins the right to a wand is indeed a noble cause, these creatures clearly aren't allowed this right for a reason. Verdict: No, the Ministry has no clue as to how these creatures think, and giving them wands would not only set a dangerous precedent, but could possibly endanger wizards and Muggles alike.

Which character would have the more interesting Pensieve: Dumbledore or Sirius Black?

Once a character dies, so do their memories—with the exception of the ones left behind in a Pensieve. These two late and beloved characters led very interesting lives—whose memories would you rather see?

Sirius Black

It would be hilarious to dive into the Pensieve and see all the pranks the Marauders pulled when they were at Hogwarts. Luckily, you wouldn't have to worry about Lupin taking a bite out of you. We would likely see memories from the Marauders' Animagi training and maybe even witness how Padfoot tricked Snape into the tunnel. Sirius might have stored fond memories of him and his best mate, James, flying around on the motorcycle during the summers they spent together. Could we see Sirius's bachelor pad at last? For that matter, what was it really like at Grimmauld Place when Sirius's parents and Regulus were still alive? Did Sirius really pin up those pictures of Muggle girls in swimsuits? Glimpsing into the Pensieve of Sirius Black would be rewarding and would answer a lot of questions about a character that departed us far too soon.

Albus Dumbledore

We have a version of Dumbledore's life story in Rita Skeeter's horrible book, *The Life and Lies of Albus Dumbledore*, but peering into his Pensieve would show the real truth. We might discover what really happened when his sister Ariana died and more about why Dumbledore held himself responsible. Maybe we'd see a more *graphic* account of what *really* happened between Dumbledore and Grindelwald when they were young. ;) And then there are all the years of his life at Hogwarts, meeting generations of students and teachers, and becoming partners with Nicholas Flamel. Just what are the twelve uses of dragon's blood anyway? You can learn so much more from a Pensieve than a Chocolate Frog Card.

Verdict

Would it be better to ride down memory lane on the back of a flying motorcycle or to visit Godric's Hollow when Dumbledore was a boy? Sirius had a great time with the three Marauders, but Dumbledore knew them too, as well as everyone else in the wizarding world for one hundred years. His depth and longevity give him the advantage. Verdict: Dumbledore's Pensieve would be the most intriguing.

Appendix

Should J.K. Rowling have kept Dumbledore's sexual orientation private?
Although the crowd at Carnegie Hall... [DH, p. 22]
J.K.R. tried to put the rumor to... [DH, p. 178]

Did Harry Potter die in Deathly Hallows?
Voldemort took the blood... [GoF, p. 642]
Harry had already figured out... [DH, p. 707]
The horrible baby under... [GoF, p. 640]
The trip to "King's... [OotP, p. 861] [DH, p. 698]
Since Harry isn't very religious... [DH, p. 706]
It is all very secret and... [DH, p. 722]

Are the Slytherins too demonized?
Yet the Prince's Tale... [DH, p. 665]
Harry doesn't know that... [HBP, p. 651]
He had Slytherin pride... [DH, p. 195]
Slytherins can be very emotional... [DH, p. 641]
But since Draco... [HBP, p. 592]
Admittedly, it's too bad... [JKR-PC2]
The actions of the... [DH, p. 631] [DH, p. 610]
By the end... [DH, p. 758]
Despite what J.K.R.... [JKR-PC2]
It's not his fault... [DH, p. 673]
We learn in the Epilogue... [DH, p. 758]
People from "worthy" houses... [DH, p. 577]
The scene where the ... [DH, p. 610]
Whatever J.K.R. said... [DH, p. 734]
Meanwhile, in SS... [SS, p. 164] [PoA, p. 139]
In Harry's first year... [SS, p. 306]

Snape has the unfortunate... [GoF, p. 101] [SS, p. 185] [CoS, p. 191]
Luna Lovegood is odd... [OotP, p. 185]
In DH, he first... [DH, p. 196]
Also, in DH... [DH, p. 726]
Snape loved Lily... [DH, p. 677]
But he came across as... [HBP, p. 497]
And then there's... [HBP, p. 213]
Harry and Ginny... [HBP, p. 146]

What is the coolest Deathly Hallow?
Though the Elder Wand... [DH, p. 718]
Draco couldn't bring ... [HBP, p. 584]
Voldemort loved killing... [DH, p. 656] [DH, p. 744]
The Elder Wand can be... [DH, p. 720]
But Harry never truly... [DH, p. 698]
The spirits of Harry's loved ones... [DH, p. 699]
Unlike the original Peverell... [DH, p. 409]
It is the only Deathly Hallow... . [SS, p. 202]
While the Resurrection Stone... [PoA, p. 347] [PoA, p. 358]
It's great for avoiding... [SS, p. 211] [GoF, p. 471]
According to Dumbledore... [SS, p. 299]
The Cloak is also great... [PoA, p. 283]
The first owner of the Cloak... [DH, p. 409]
However, Harry wisely put... [DH, p. 749]
It's awe-inspiring, but sad... [DH, p. 748]

Is the Epilogue a letdown?
For instance, it's great to know... [DH, p. 757]
J.K.R. had all the answers... [JKR-BC]
Nineteen years laster... [DH, p. 755]
To his credit, Harry... [DH, p. 758]
These questions were raised... [JKR-OS]
Draco's Child Scorpius... [DH, p. 756]

Which character fails to live up to expectations?
He shows up at Christmas... [HBP, p. 334]
He could have been the coolest... [PoA, p. 381]

If he really loved... [HBP, p. 624]

It's obvious that married life... [DH, p. 214]

But, by then, readers have lost... [DH, p. 514]

Lupin has a few great... [PoA, p. 237] [OotP, p. 47] [OotP, p. 807]

While it's true that... [DH, p. 661]

The last time we see him... [DH, p. 700]

That is a shame, considering... [OotP, p. 49]

She falls apart when... [HBP, p. 467]

Tonks was a Metamorphmagus... [OotP, p. 52]

So it fell short of expectations... [HBP, p. 465]

Her hair turned from passionate... [HBP, p. 157] [HBP, p. 160]

Who (besides Voldemort) is the character you hate the most?

He's a horrible father-figure... [SS, p. 36]

He makes sure the neighbors... [PoA, p. 24]

Vernon's worst trait... [OotP, p. 4]

But at least when Vern... [OotP, p. 41]

Talk about denial—after Voldemort... [OotP, p. 217]

In OotP, he also installs his protégé... [OotP, p. 308]

Fudge favors the wealthy and racist... [GoF, p. 708]

As bad people go... [DH, p. 573] [OotP, p. 265]

But Snape actually... [CoS, p. 173] [OotP, p. 364] [HBP, p. 532]

Who is the better supporting character: Luna Lovegood or Neville Longbottom?

She is an outcast when... [OotP, p. 185]

She is also Ginny Weasley's... [HBP, p. 413]

Although she definitely supports... [OotP, p. 683] [OotP, p. 403]

Luna's like a mystical princess... [DH, p. 464] [DH, p.480]

Neville's grandmother cares about... [OotP, p. 707]

Frank Longbottom was an Auror... [Ootp, p. 514]

So Neville is a survivor... [PoA, p. 137] [OotP, p. 800]

He also isn't afraid to cross... [SS, p. 272]

In DH, Neville could have... [DH, p. 574]

Instead, Neville stood up... [DH, p. 575] [DH, p. 580] [DH, p. 731]

With his kind nature and love... [DH, p. 733]

What duel is the best in the series?

It occurs after Harry... [GoF, p. 636]

And, of course, the Noseless One... [GoF, p. 660]

But from the minute the real dueling... [GoF, p. 663]

To the surprise of the Death Eater... [SS, p. 85]

Even Harry's dead parents... [GoF, p. 667]

Nobody dies or even gets hurt... [DH, p. 698]

What the Dark Lord didn't know... [DH, p. 655]

Fawkes the phoenix shows up... [DH, p. 719]

The best duel is the one... [DH, p. 736]

She is standing up for Gideon... [OotP, p. 174] [JKR-OS]

She's also grieving the loss... [DH, p. 661]

She's especially scared for... [CoS, p. 309]

Bellatrix has also gone after... [OotP, p. 783]

That happened just before... [OotP, p. 805]

Bellatrix apparently dumps... [JKR-CH]

Molly, on the other hand... [CoS, p. 59] [OotP, p. 98] [HBP, p. 82]

As Harry evokes the names... [DH, p. 739]

It's absolutely Harry's duel to lose... [DH, p. 743]

He uses good old *Expelliarmus*... [DH, p. 743]

Who helps Harry more on his quest: Ron or Hermione?

Harry sees a kindred soul... [SS, p. 101]

But whenever Harry really needs... [OotP, p. 219]

Because Hermione's mind is... [SS, p. 283]

At least he remembers... [SS, p. 278]

Ron is useless at helping... [SS, p. 220]

Who has the idea... [OotP, p. 326]

Who knows that the Half-Blood... [HBP, p. 239]

And who rescues... [DH, p. 423]

Ron just can't multitask... [GoF, p. 287] [OotP, p. 796] [HBP, p. 397]

Ron runs away... [DH, p. 310]

Hermione is with... [DH, p. 327]

It's really unfair... [DH, p. 349]

What is the most shocking moment in the series?

When Voldemort tried... [GoF, p. 653]

Voldemort's most faithful... [JKR-PC1]
Peter nurses the horrible... [GoF, p. 7]
Cousin Bellatrix gets in... [OotP, p. 806]
Maybe Harry would figure... [OotP, p. 858]
But then, in that... [HBP, p. 595]

Which character is most surprising?
In fact, the crusty, old... [GoF, p. 682]
So when Professor Moody... [GoF, p. 213]
When he is nice... [GoF, p. 595]
The real Moody... [GoF, p. 681]
In fact, Snape never was... [HBP, p. 26] [HBP, p. 588]
He's Dumbledore's man... [DH, p. 683]
And, of course, Lily... [DH, p. 678] [DH, p. 689]
When Harry sees... [DH, p. 740]
The catalyst for change... [OotP, p. 851]
But it all backfires... [HBP, p. 522]
Trying to become a murderer... [HBP, p. 585]
Draco never wants... [HBP, p. 592]
He doesn't seem too thrilled... [DH, p. 11]
And more importantly... [DH, p. 459]
That's especially amazing... [HBP, p. 522]
In HBP, she sees the good... [HBP, p. 34]
She has no love... [HBP, p. 114]
But, in the end... [DH, p. 726]
When Aunt Petunia... [DH, p. 40]

Should the love potion Amortentia be illegal?
Dumbledore refers to the relationship... [HBP, p. 214]
That's not very different... [GoF, p. 213]
It's true that Merope... [HBP, p. 214]
Look what happens... [HBP, p. 391]
J.K.R. said during... [JKR-PC2]
If it was so bad... [HBP, p. 186]
Why would it have... [HBP, p. 183]
Molly Weasley laughingly... [PoA, p. 70]
He actually hurts Hermione's... [HBP, p. 302]

She has no friends... [HBP, p. 210]
As singer Celestina... [HBP, p. 330]

What is the most useful potion?
If someone has luck... [HBP, p. 187]
With it, he is able... [HBP, p. 490]
Even the very thought... [HBP, p. 299]
Professor Slughorn also tells... [HBP, p. 187]
Harry is able to generously... [HBP, p. 552]
Felix Felicis may be... [HBP, p. 187]
But even a child can make... [CoS, p. 215]
And you don't want... [CoS, p. 226]
Sure, we see abuses... [GoF, p. 680] [HBP, p. 457]
Harry and the Trio... [DH, p. 237] [DH, p. 523]
The best use... [DH, p. 50]

Which is the best book?
At the Quidditch World... [GoF, p. 82]
Later in the Tri-wizard... [GoF, p. 250]
There's a dance called... [GoF, p. 397]

Is Dumbledore right that Hogwarts "sorts too soon"?
And the Sorting Hat... [SS, p. 121]
Look at Peter Pettigrew... [PoA, p. 369]
On the opposite side... [OotP, p. 112]
Young Snape thinks... [DH, p. 672]
Harry is told by Hagrid... [SS, p. 80]
Hermione could have been... [SS, p. 106]
He wants to be... [DH, p. 672]
And Lily loyally stands... [DH, p. 674]
Later, when Harry's... [DH, p. 758]
The hat gives Peter... [PoA, p. 207]
The other Slytherins... [CoS, p. 195]
But the Sorting Hat... [CoS, p. 333]
Look at Neville... [SS, p. 120]
Lily and Snape... [DH, p. 676]

What is the most useful magical object for preserving history?
They can move... [GoF, p. 284]

The portraits have a job... [OotP, p. 473]

When Mr. Weasley... [OotP, p. 469]

The human portraits... [PoA, p. 160]

Later, the painting... [OotP, p. 473]

But Phineas is also... [OotP, p. 826]

He moves between... [OotP, p. 496]

His role is that... [DH, p. 689]

So that brings us... [DH, p. 689]

Without the help... [DH, p. 569]

Mrs. Black's painting... [OotP, p. 78] [GoF, p. 432]

Sir Cadogan... [PoA, p. 100]

Harry learns in GoF... [GoF, p. 597]

It's not like... [SS, p. 213]

By splashing down... [GoF, p. 594]

When Harry is older... [OotP, p. 841]

Through the saved-up... [HBP, p. 269]

Without the useful... [OotP, p. 646]

The memories in... [DH, p. 662]

Are the female characters too stereotyped?
Molly Weasley scolds... [OotP, p. 87]

Mrs. Black's Portrait... [OotP, p. 180]

In DH, all of Hermione's... [DH, p. 312]

She is locked up... [DH, p. 627]

Harry later releases her... [DH, p. 736]

No matter what happens... [OotP, p. 52]

Luna isn't just... [HBP, p. 311]

Cho Chang talks... [OotP, p. 561]

How is Hermione... [DH, p. 313]

It's true that Tonks... [OotP, p. 158] [OotP, p. 498]

And remember—Tonks... [DH, p. 10]

She doesn't let anything... [DH, p. 736]

Caring for magical children... [SS, p. 25]

When Madam Trelawney hurls... [DH, p. 646]

Neither is Madam... [QA, p. viii] [OotP, p. 20] [GoF, p. 685]

Harry couldn't have defeated... [DH, p. 726]

Is the final duel between Harry and Voldemort a disappointment?
Harry knows he is... [DH, p. 743]
Obviously, one... [OotP, p. 844]
The word mundane... [DH, p. 744]
But the Elder Wand... [DH, p. 743]

Who would win in a fight: Dumbledore or Gandalf?
Dumbledore has no... [HBP, p. 503]
Dumbledore is so pitiful... [HBP, p. 569]
He has one good... [OotP, p. 813]
Even in the afterlife... [DH, p. 713]
Voldemort never comes... [SS, p. 102]
In HBP, Dumbledore... [HBP, p. 576]

Would the series be stronger if Voldemort had killed Harry?
J.K.R. wrote that... [JKR-OS]
And what about... [SS, p. 297]
In DH, Harry is... [DH, p. 739]
Even Voldemort taunts... [DH, p. 660]
And according to... [DH, p. 753]

Is Severus Snape a hero?
According to Dumbledore... [HBP, p. 548]
What Snape really wants... [DH, p. 677]
There is no heroism... [SS, p. 138]
No good guy... [GoF, p. 300]
Snape taunts Sirius... [OotP, p. 520] [PoA, p. 423]
In HBP... [HBP, p. 36]
He is insulting... [OotP, p. 672]
In DH, Snape took... [DH, p. 370]
As headmaster... [DH, p. 575]
As seen through... [DH, p. 678]
Voldemort only gives... [DH, p. 677]
Snape has two choices... [DH, p. 678]
That is why he... [GoF, p. 713]

Snape's only motivation... [DH, p. 687]
He protects the secrets... [DH, p. 688]
Also, in DH, Harry... [DH, p. 680]
Harry says plainly... [DH, p. 758]

Is S.P.E.W. good or bad for house-elves?
Hermione starts... [GoF, p. 239]
Remember the creepy... [OotP, p. 62]
Unfortunately, Hermione goes about... [OotP, p. 255]
She convinces Harry... [OotP, p. 832]
Instead of having him... [HBP, p. 52] [DH, p. 198]

Which character is more underestimated by others: Kreacher or Peter Pettigrew?
Maybe it's the fact... [OotP, p. 504] [OotP, p. 108]
Sirius Black treats... [OotP, p. 109]
Yet Sirius takes... [OotP, p. 504]
That is a huge... [OotP, p. 834]
Later in DH... [DH, p. 198]
Sirius never thinks... [DH, p. 192]
Voldemort makes the same... [DH, p. 195]
Good thing, too... [DH, p. 219]
And then he leads... [DH, p. 734]
Professor McGonagall... [PoA, p. 207] [PoA, p. 369]
As Sirius explains... [PoA, p. 368]
Peter blows up... [PoA, p. 208]
Yep—the underestimated... [PoA, p. 350]
Harry shows him mercy... [PoA, p. 381]
When we next see... [GoF, p. 7]
By the time he cuts... [GoF, p. 642]
In "Snape's Worst Memory"... [OotP, p. 646]

Is it appropriate for Harry to use Unforgivable Curses?
And to slow her... [OotP, p. 810]
Yes, it's true that... [GoF, p. 212]
And there is a sense... [GoF, p. 603]
The boy can't have... [DH, p. 683]

When Amycus Carrow... [DH, p. 593]
But hey—all is fair... [DH, p. 575]
After all, when Molly... [DH, p. 737]
Also, having been the victim... [GoF, p. 661]
In the Battle of the Tower... [HBP, p. 398]
Plus, there are other... [OotP, p. 789]
At the end... [PoA, p. 375]
The most depressing... [DH, p. 593]
And what's really crazy... [HBP, p. 598]
Several times in DH Harry... [DH, p. 655]

Which of the scenes from the books should the filmmakers have left in the movies?
A lot of readers were... [PoA, p. 131]

Who would you like to know better: Andromeda Tonks or Blaise Zabini?
Sirius Black calls... [OotP, p. 113]
We know she was... [HBP, p. 70]
Andromeda's daughter... [OotP, p. 52]
It's interesting that... [DH, p. 66]
After the fall... [DH, p. 756]
His name is called out... [SS, p. 122] [HBP, p. 150]
Pansy Parkinson teases... [HBP, p. 149]
At the meeting... [HBP, p. 145]
Blaise shows curiosity... [HBP, p. 152]

If you could go back in time and talk J.K. Rowling into changing something in the books, what would you change?
It would have been... [DH, p. 678]
It would just be... [DH, p. 655]

Is Xenophilius Lovegood a traitor?
In DH, he tried to sell... [DH, p. 421]
Even if he was Obliviated... [DH, p. 422]
Her empty bedroom... [DH, p. 418]
When Mr. Lovegood blocks... [DH, p. 419]
Since Harry helps Luna... [DH, p. 468]

Whose death is the saddest?
After an exciting youth... [PoA, p. 208]
Sirius is sent... [PoA, p. 371]
The time Harry... [OotP, p. 84]
In OotP, Harry is tricked... [OotP, p. 781]
And then she strikes... [OotP, p. 806]
But in DH, when Harry used... [DH, p. 699]
Since Dumbledore is friends... [SS, p. 220]
So readers can't accept... [HBP, p. 503] [DH, p. 681]
Toward the end... [HBP, p. 576]
He would have died... [HBP, p. 577] [DH, p. 683]
They both have to watch... [HBP, p. 596]
Alas, he was really dead... [DH, p. 713]
As his final act... [DH, p. 476]
The other children... [DH, p. 480]
He has one of... [DH, p. 657]
And later Harry realizes... [DH, p. 687]
Dumbledore never means... [DH, p. 721]

Should Voldemort be pitied or loathed?
Dumbledore and Slughorn... [CoS, p. 247]
He even hunts down... [GoF, p. 3] [HBP, p. 502]
Young Tom Riddle... [HBP, p. 203] [HBP, p. 262]
His nature was bent... [HBP, p. 273]

Should Harry have chosen a different profession than Auror?
Harry also realizes in OotP... [OotP, p. 620]
Harry would rather be... [DH, p. 440]

What is the worst book?
Even on the day...[OotP, p. 65,66]
Maybe he is taking...[OotP, p. 83]
Housecleaning with Molly...[OotP, p. 117]
Unlike cooking scenes...[OotP, p. 96]
It's also depressing that...[OotP, p. 481]
No joke—that's probably...[OotP, p. 716]
We are served...[OotP, p. 416]

Harry meets the luminescent...[OotP, p. 185][OotP, p. 392]
Snape and Harry clash...[OotP, p. 651]
Hagrid brings home...[OotP, p. 691]
Again somebody dies...[OotP, p. 806]
He has a tantrum...[OotP, p. 824]
The big secret Dumbledore...[OotP, p. 841]
Half of the book takes...[CoS, p. 156]
Harry is flush...[CoS, p. 200]
When Harry and Ron...[CoS, p. 79]
The giant spiders...[CoS, p. 266]
Sadly, Dumbledore never...[CoS, p. 180]
All the Headmaster would...[CoS, p. 315]
There's another major flaw...[SS, p. 28]
Even Aragog the spider...[CoS, p. 278]
So it wasn't really...[CoS, p. 144]
Tom Riddle pulls one...[CoS, p. 312]

Are the Hufflepuffs dismissed as lame?

Even the cute Auror... [HBP, p. 82]
Not only is she... [PoA, p. 166] [OotP, p. 606]
Take Justin-Finch Fletchly... [CoS, p. 194] [CoS, p. 202]
Susan Bones is mentioned... [OotP, p. 350]
Ernie McMillan... [DH, p. 649]
Zacharias Smith is... [HBP, p. 147]
But, even worse... [DH, p. 613]
She's a symbol of Hufflepuff... [HBP, p. 435]
Tonks is a cool... [DH, p. 624]
And remember Cedric Diggory? [GoF, p. 634]
As for Hepzibah... [HBP, p. 437]
It's true that Zacharias... [OotP, p. 217]

Are the Gryffindors too glorified?

The same could be said... [HBP, p. 191]
But no one would say... [PoA, p. 367]
He may have sought... [DH, p. 470]
Ginny Weasley is... [HBP, p. 146]
Finally, there is Dumbledore... [DH, p. 357]

Harry's parents were... [DH, p. 672]
And look at all... [DH, p. 755]
James and Sirius... [OotP, p. 648]
Yet, they were never punished... [SS, p. 55]
The twins are just as irreverant... [GoF, p. 49]
Their little sister... [HBP, p. 298]
Hermione underhandedly helps... [HBP, p. 232]
Then in the Epilogue... [DH, p. 755]
Even Neville's gran... [DH, p. 624]

What is the best plotline in the books?

It's a persuasive... [DH, p. 678]
To the young teenage... [PoA, p. 283]
GoF added another layer... [GoF, p. 519]
GoF finally opens... [GoF, p. 590]
At the end of the book... [GoF, p. 679]
So J.K.R. was almost... [GoF, p. 300] [GoF, p. 209]
In OotP and HBP... [OotP, p. 646]
Since Snape and Sirius... [HBP, p. 161] [OotP, p. 832]
As HBP goes along... [HBP, p. 588]
Seen through adult eyes... [DH, p. 678]
He cares about Dumbledore... [DH, p. 689]
It's not a surprise... [DH, p. 758]
Unlike the plotline... [SS, p. 15]
Readers see Horcruxes... [CoS, p. 322]
Each Horcrux holds... [DH, p. 103]
And even though Harry... [HBP, p. 506]
Harry destroys Tom Riddle's... [HBP, p. 503]
It's about a murderer... [HBP, p. 506]
Harry has to come... [DH, p. 478]

Does the Secret-Keeper information revealed in Deathly Hallows contradict the previous rules about Secret-Keepers?

Peter Pettigrew was... [PoA, p. 369]
And again, in OotP... [OotP, p. 58]
Arthur Weasley tells... [DH, p. 90]
But when a Death Eater... [DH, p. 270]

But Bill Weasley... [DH, p. 482]
That's why Harry... [OotP, p. 58]
Dumbledore even said... [HBP, p. 50]

Are Harry and Hermione partly responsible for Snape's death since they never tried to save his life?

There was nothing... [DH, p. 655]
Why does he forget... [HBP, p. 638]
She never hated Snape... [PoA, p. 377]

Which couple has the most romantic story?

Even before that, they met... [JKR-OS]
Their first kiss... [HBP, p 533]
Soon Ginny is... [HBP, p. 536]
After a lonely... [DH, p. 753]
These two get off... [SS, p. 175]
Even so, Ron nearly... [GoF, p. 404]
Even in HBP... [HBP, p. 352]
Sometimes true love... [HBP, p. 393] [HBP, p. 313]
Their darkest hour... [DH, p. 310]
Ron realizes that... [DH, p. 384]

Who would win in a fight: centaurs or giants?

While it's true... [OotP, p. 759]

Besides Voldemort, who is the worst villain?

It's Lucius who... [CoS, p. 63]
In PoA, he tries... [PoA, p. 218]
His sinister plot... [OotP, p. 781]
Even after spending time... [DH, p. 8]
The word beast... [HBP, 593]
He preys on small... [HBP, 334]
He bit and turned... [HBP, p. 335] [HBP, p. 622] [DH, p.465]

Should Parseltongue be taught at Hogwarts?

If Ron can learn... [DH, p. 623]

Harry doesn't exactly enjoy... [CoS, p. 198]
In the Epilogue... [DH, p. 755]

Do the life debts really matter?
Harry saves Dudley's... [DH, p. 40]
Snape owes at least... [SS, p. 300] [DH, p. 678]
Harry in his turn... [DH, p. 470]
Dumbledore offers... [DH, p. 459]
Harry frees Dobby... [CoS, p. 338] [DH, p. 477]
He goes along... [GoF, p. 642]

Is the Snitch worth too many points in Quidditch?
When a Seeker... [SS, p. 169]
At the Quidditch World... [GoF, p. 113]

Would you rather have Harry's Invisibility Cloak or his Firebolt flying broomstick?
But, of course, this is... [DH, p. 409]
Accelerating 0-150... [PoA, p. 51]

Who would be the scariest mom: Rita Skeeter or Dolores Umbridge?
Imagine the fear... [GoF, p. 304]
It's frightening just... [OotP, p. 266]

Should goblins and house-elves be allowed to carry wands?
Hermione is convinced... [GoF, p. 239]
Plus, they would... [GoF, p. 136]
Dobby sure as hell... [CoS, p. 338] [DH, p. 473]
As for goblins... [DH, p. 505]

Which character would have the more interesting Pensieve: Dumbledore or Sirius Black?
We have a version... [DH, p. 353]
And then there are ... [SS, p. 103]

About the Authors

Emerson Spartz is the founder of MuggleNet.com, a website that receives 15 million hits per month and is the most popular *Harry Potter* website on the Internet. Spartz, now twenty-two, created the website at age twelve and now manages a staff of 120. In the summer of 2006, *Harry Potter* author J.K. Rowling invited Spartz to her house in Scotland for a private interview. He is currently studying business at the University of Notre Dame.

Nineteen-year-old **Ben Schoen** has co-managed MuggleNet.com with Emerson since 2003. He is a host on MuggleCast, MuggleNet's world-renowned podcast, reaching over 70,000 subscribers. In 2007, Schoen, along with Spartz, co-authored the *New York Times* bestselling book *MuggleNet.com's What Will Happen in Harry Potter 7*. He is currently studying psychology/sociology at the University of Notre Dame.

Jeanne Kimsey has been a member of MuggleNet's official Chamber of Secrets forum since 2003, and is also essay moderator for the Harry Potter Network. She lives in Tennessee where she is writing her Slytherin-themed blog Rattlesnakeroot.